NITYANANDA
In Divine Presence

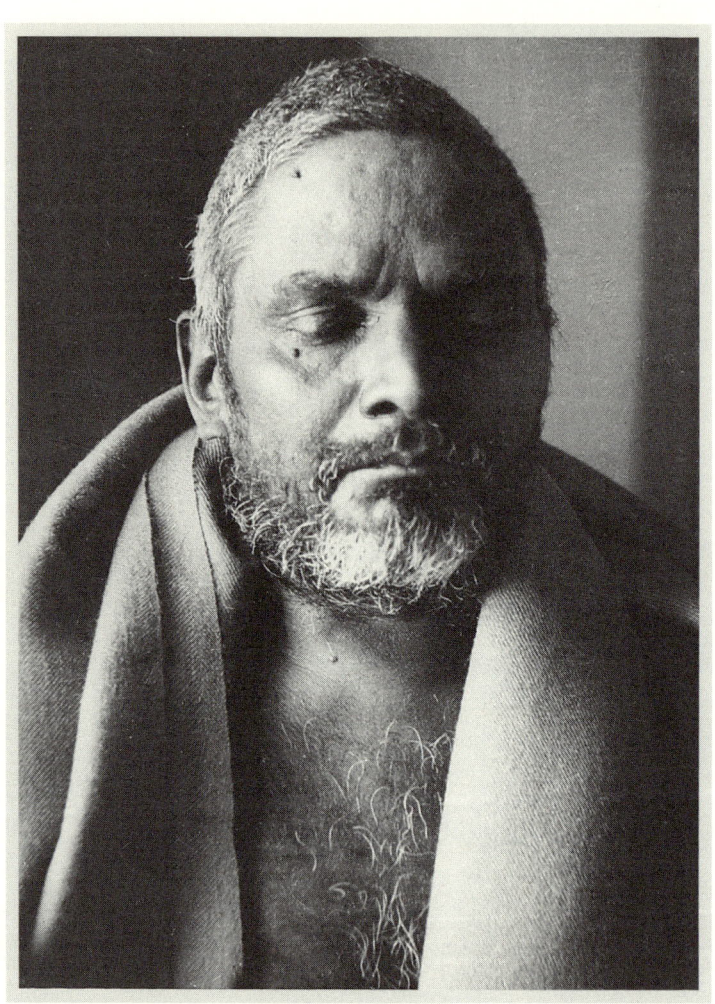

NITYANANDA
In Divine Presence

by Swami Chetanananda
and M.U. Hatengdi

RUDRA PRESS Portland, Oregon

Rudra Press
PO Box 13310
Portland, Oregon 97213
Telephone: (503) 231-0346
Telefax: (503) 236-9878
www.rudrapress.com
email: rudrapress@comcast.net

© 1998, Swami Chetanananda
All rights reserved. First edition 1998.
Printed in the United States of America.

No part of this publication may be used or reproduced in any manner whatsoever without written permission, except in the case of brief quotations embodied in critical articles and reviews.

Book and cover design: Bill Stanton
Photographs: M.D. Suvarna
Editor: Cheryl Berling Rosen

Chetanananda, Swami.
   Nityananda : In Divine Presence / by Swami Chetanananda and M.U. Hatengdi.
      p. cm.
   ISBN 978-0-915801-76-3 (alk. paper)
   1. Nityananda, Swami, 1897-1961. 2. Hindus--India--Biography.
I. Hatengdi, M.U., 1914-   . II. Title.
BL1175.N48C54   1998
294.5'513'092--dc21   97-51368
[B]   CIP

The great Vedantist philosopher Shankara, on composing the hymn *Soundarya Lahari* in praise of the Universal Mother, wrote:

To praise Her is like waving a light before the Sun made of its own flame

Like offering oblation to the Moon from drops oozing from the Moonstone

Or like satisfying the Ocean with its own water

With like words, we dedicate this work to Nityananda's divine Grace.

—*Swami Chetanananda and Captain M.U. Hatengdi*

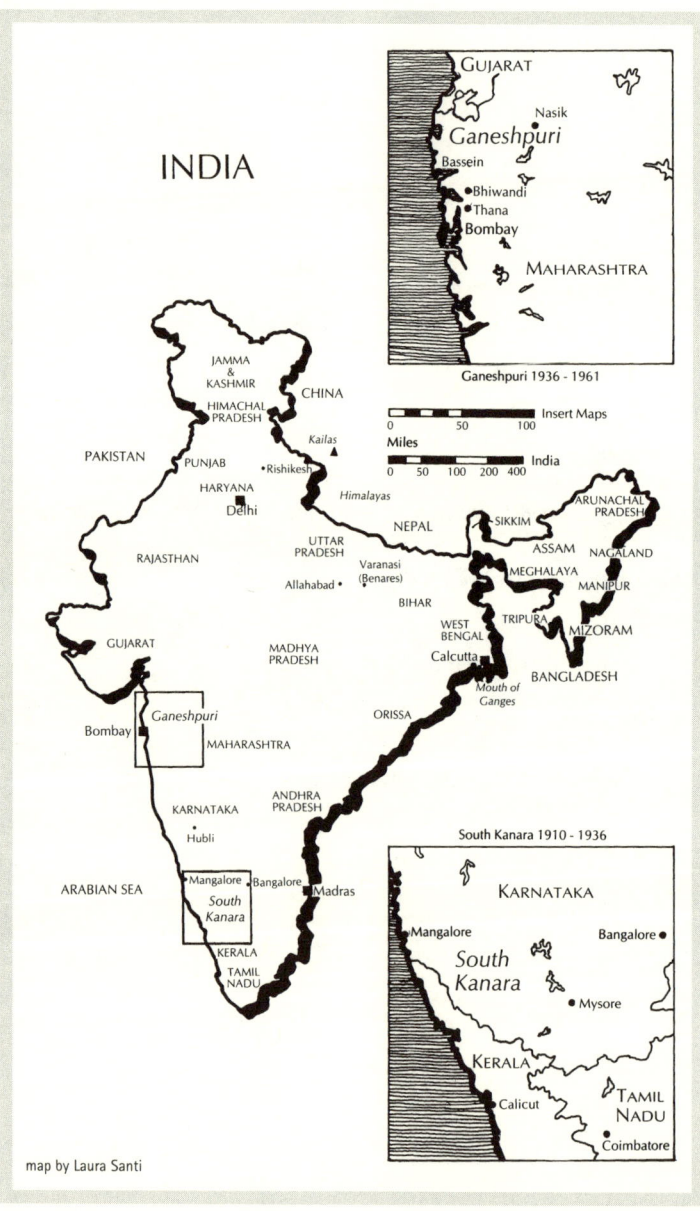

Contents

	Foreword by Swami Chetanananda	ix
	Preface by M.U. Hatengdi	xiii
	Introduction by Swami Chetanananda	xv
ONE	Remembering the Master	1
TWO	The Early Years 1900–1915	13
THREE	South Kanara 1915–1936	19
FOUR	Discovery in Udipi 1918	27
FIVE	The Mangalore Days of Rail Travel 1923–1933	37
SIX	Kanhangad's Rock Ashram 1925–1936	45
SEVEN	Ganeshpuri—The Beginning 1936	55
EIGHT	The Old Ashram 1936–1950	61
NINE	The Old Ashram 1950–1956	83
TEN	The New Ashram at Kailas 1956–1961	95
ELEVEN	Nityananda's Passing August 8, 1961	111
TWELVE	Afterword	127
	Glossary	137

FOREWORD

During a trip to India in 1973, I visited the samadhi temple of Nityananda. To reach Ganeshpuri, the rural town where he lived for over thirty years and established an ashram, I hired a taxi. The driver assured me he knew the way, having been there several times. And when he learned it was my first visit, he told the following story:

> As a young man he heard that a great saint lived in Ganeshpuri and decided to go there to receive his blessing. Arriving, he stepped into a line several hours long because, at this point in Nityananda's life, thousands of people came to see him every day. When at last he drew near enough to see the saint, he observed him saying very little. One by one, the people in line would bow and offer a gift of some sort or ask a question. Nityananda always replied simply, sometimes with only a gesture or sound. Therefore when my taxi driver's turn came, he was quite startled to hear Nityananda say, "Go and bring your brother here." Aware of the saint's healing powers, he dutifully returned the following week with his brother who had been blind since birth. This time Nityananda told him to leave his brother at the ashram, go home, and come back in three days. Again he followed the instructions and, returning on the given day, saw his brother smiling at him. He could see!

I had the good fortune in India to hear many stories about Nityananda—stories that reflected his simplicity, his austerity, his detachment from the world, and his pure and powerful love for those who came to him. The more I heard, the more I recognized two things. First of all, they deserved a larger audience. Secondly, these stories were the most powerful and direct way to express the essence of his very extraordinary presence. I decided to gather as many stories as I could, and began to travel along the route that Nityananda followed—from Cannanore in the south, through Mangalore and Kanhangad, and finally to Ganeshpuri. Along the way, I met many people who had known him directly or whose parents had known him. Their remarkable and moving narratives confirmed my sense of what an exceptional being Nityananda was as well as how rich a collection of stories about him would be.

Now, saints or gurus often bewilder both their followers and others who hear about them. Their words can be confusing, their actions peculiar, their knowledge and insight contrary to the precepts of logic. These things can cause consternation and even doubt. We see this over and over in the recorded lives of all great spiritual beings—from Jesus to the Buddha, from Moses to Mohammed. However, it is the infinite mystery surrounding such people that compels their disciples and devotees to try to capture their inexpressible presence in order to inspire others. And so stories are told...

Nityananda's life was no exception to this rule. Much of what he did was enigmatic, his behavior often startling even his closest devotees. But everything he touched was uplifted. Whether indirectly, through totally unpredictable circumstances, or years later, Nityananda's actions benefited the seeker—even if he or she came with base motives. Story after story testifies to this.

Throughout 1979 and 1980 I was collecting these stories of Nityananda with the help of Swami Prajnananda, Swami Muktananda's assistant, who greatly encouraged me and provided a list of contacts. I learned then of M.U. Hatengdi and an earlier book he had written. As a long-standing devotee of Nityananda, Captain Hatengdi not only had personal recollections to relate but knew others who had directly experienced Nityananda's presence. Visiting him in Bombay, I recognized an extraordinary opportunity to accomplish my mission. Together we agreed to combine forces.

The stories that follow paint the portrait of a remarkable being. It is an intimate portrait because, upon reading them, we can easily feel his presence. As far as it is possible to reveal any divine mystery, these tales reveal that of Nityananda. As far as it is possible to capture spiritual grace, they capture his. As far as it is possible to put words to the Divine, they testify to his divinity. With pleasure and profound gratitude, we present this book.

Swami Chetanananda

PREFACE

After writing a few articles on the great Master of Ganeshpuri, friends who were likewise devotees from the early days pressed me to attempt his life story. Mrs. M. Krishnabai was the first to urge me to undertake this service. However, I was unable to obtain the information and assistance I needed to fulfill my ideal of a biography of Nityananda. Only a few well-authenticated incidents have been recorded and there were certain to be many omissions.

My project was aided by a chance meeting with Mr. R. B. Bellare of Bandra in September 1980. Motivated by his desire to make some contribution, his zeal, efficiency, and regularity made this small tribute possible.

This is the first book I am aware of that presents Nityananda to English-speaking readers in an authentic setting. I was particularly gratified by Swami Chetanananda's proposal to publish it in the United States. I gratefully acknowledge the staff of the Nityananda Institute and Rudra Press for their dedicated effort and unflagging zeal in editing my original manuscript in order to present Nityananda to the American reader in clear, understandable language, without any unnecessary frills.

My aim will be more than fulfilled if this book aids the reader, to even the smallest extent, in exploring and experiencing the wonder of the Master known as Nityananda.

M.U. Hatengdi

Introduction

In Nityananda's awe-inspiring presence was the heart of a compassionate mother. Already a full-fledged master in his teens and twenties, he may have been speaking of himself when he compared *sadhus*,[1] or seekers of truth, to the jackfruit, whose forbidding exterior yields a honeyed sweetness when opened. From his earliest known days to the final ones in Ganeshpuri, his presence provided a sense of security for the poor and those in distress. It also gave hope to spiritual aspirants. People from all walks of life came for his blessing—yogis and renunciates, scholars and artists, politicians and civil servants, other saints and spiritual teachers. They were rich and poor, strong and sick; they came from all over India and the rest of the world.

Much about Nityananda's life remains unclear. Stories abound that put him in different places at the same time, resulting in considerable confusion about his true age or background. Not unexpectedly, his devotees listened careful-

---

1. A glossary of Sanskrit terms is at the end of this book.

ly for clues or details because occasionally in casual conversation Nityananda would touch upon some incident from his past. However, he always cut short attempts to obtain details and admonished those who persisted. Some recall him making passing references to visiting Ceylon and Singapore while others say he displayed an intimate knowledge of the Himalayan region. It is said he spoke of being in Madras in 1902 when Swami Vivekananda attained *samadhi*.

Even his name holds a mystery. Stories of his childhood relate that his adoptive mother called him Ram. "Nityananda" means "eternal bliss" and was used to describe the state of mind he inspired. To a devotee who sat before him ecstatically repeating "nityanand, nityanand" as a mantra, he said, "It is not a name—it is a state!" In fact, early devotees called him swami, master, or sadhu while the name Nityananda was attached to him only in later years.

Clearly, a literary portrait of one such as Nityananda requires both an enormous canvas and an adept artist. Such a painting has yet to appear. Of the hundreds of thousands of people who came for his blessing, few recorded their experiences. Furthermore, Nityananda had no gospel and promoted no particular readings or spiritual practice (*sadhana*). The advice he gave to one person was not necessarily what he gave to another. He simply urged all devotees to cultivate a pure mind and an intense desire for liberation (*shuddha bhavana* and *shraddha*).

Nityananda's self-abnegation was complete. He wore nothing but a loincloth, and sometimes not even that. During his time in South Kanara, he only ate if food was brought to him. He had a total disregard for the physical elements including his nightly resting place. Unusual phenomena surrounded him naturally, including instances of actual healing. Yet he was never motivated by a desire for publicity and frowned on devotees who attributed to him experiences that we might describe as miracles. When pressed, he would call it the greatness of the location or the faith of the devout. "Everything that happens, happens automatically by the will of God," he would say.

A spiritual powerhouse, he desired only that people develop their powers to receive what he was capable of transmitting. "While the ocean has plenty of water, it is the size of the container you bring to it that determines how much you collect." Embodying what is ideal and pure, he would say, "One who sees this one once will not forget," implying that the seed of spiritual consciousness sown by his *darshan* would sprout in due course when correctly cultivated.[2] He denied having an earthly guru or a particular spiritual practice. He adopted no disciples and never intended to establish an organization—although his devotees, most of them common householders, were legion. His silent, unseen mission was to offer relief to suffering humanity, whether people came or not, and to transmit a greater consciousness to those who sought higher values. Grace emanated from his being and from his silent companionship. A lone glimpse of his personality could shatter the ego of the proud and evoke the hope and aspirations of the genuine seeker.

Those who sought him out for material success benefited while the few who came out of pure devotion found their spiritual evolution accelerated with little or no effort on their parts. Nityananda accomplished this by becoming an obsession, if I can express it that way—a divine obsession.

---

2. Nityananda never referred to himself in the first person singular, instead saying "this one" or "from here."

While living in the everyday world, devotees imbibed the spirit of the Bhagavad Gita and were gradually processed from within. They had to do very little. Seekers and other pilgrims benefited both through the arousal of their spiritual consciousness and by capably meeting life's challenges with his help. He converted their very breath into consciousness, bringing a gradual inner ripening, which in turn led to a restless longing for the Divine and a dispassion for worldly things. All this occurred without affecting the day-to-day efficiency in their chosen fields of endeavor. This is how Nityananda's grace silently worked.

His mighty spiritual force filled the South Kanara district for a few years and then moved on to Kanhangad, Gokarn, and Vajreshwari. Later he settled at Ganeshpuri, nestled at the foot of the majestic Mandakini Mountain amidst blue hills, green fields, hot springs, and the Bhimeshwar shrine. Perhaps Nityananda chose this spot to revive the holiness of this ancient spiritual center.[3]

Nityananda used to say that the true reward for genuine devotion (*bhakti*) was a still greater dose of pure desireless devotion—not material prosperity or social success. He played and still plays the role of the eternal Krishna as Gopala, tending his allegorical herd of devotees. He guides and watches them at pasture during their earthly sojourn, helps them onward, then brings them home safely as the

---

3. Legend has it that here Sri Rama's guru, Sage Vasistha, performed a special sacrificial rite (*yajna*). He created 360 hot springs so that the large number of invited sages could bathe in a different spring each day of the year to ward off the physical ailments and mental distractions being brought about by Indra, who had decided to thwart the rite. Finding that Vasistha continued despite these obstructions, Indra aimed his Vajra-Astra to destroy the rite. Mother Parvati reportedly presented herself and absorbed the weapon, thereby saving the rite. Henceforth she was installed at the spot as Vajreshwari and a shrine was erected for her. The fort-like structure that now stands there was constructed by the Peshwas, who pledged that if successful in capturing the Bassein Fort from the Portuguese they would raise a new temple to her on the old site—patterned after a fort.

evening closes on their lives, either to rest permanently in liberation (*mukti*) if they have advanced enough or to start afresh by leading them to another morning of birth in a continual process of evolution.

Nityananda was capable of granting all kinds of wishes but said only one thing was really worth the effort. "One must seek the shortest route and fastest means to get back home—to turn one's inner spark into a blaze and then to merge and identify with that greater fire which ignited the spark."

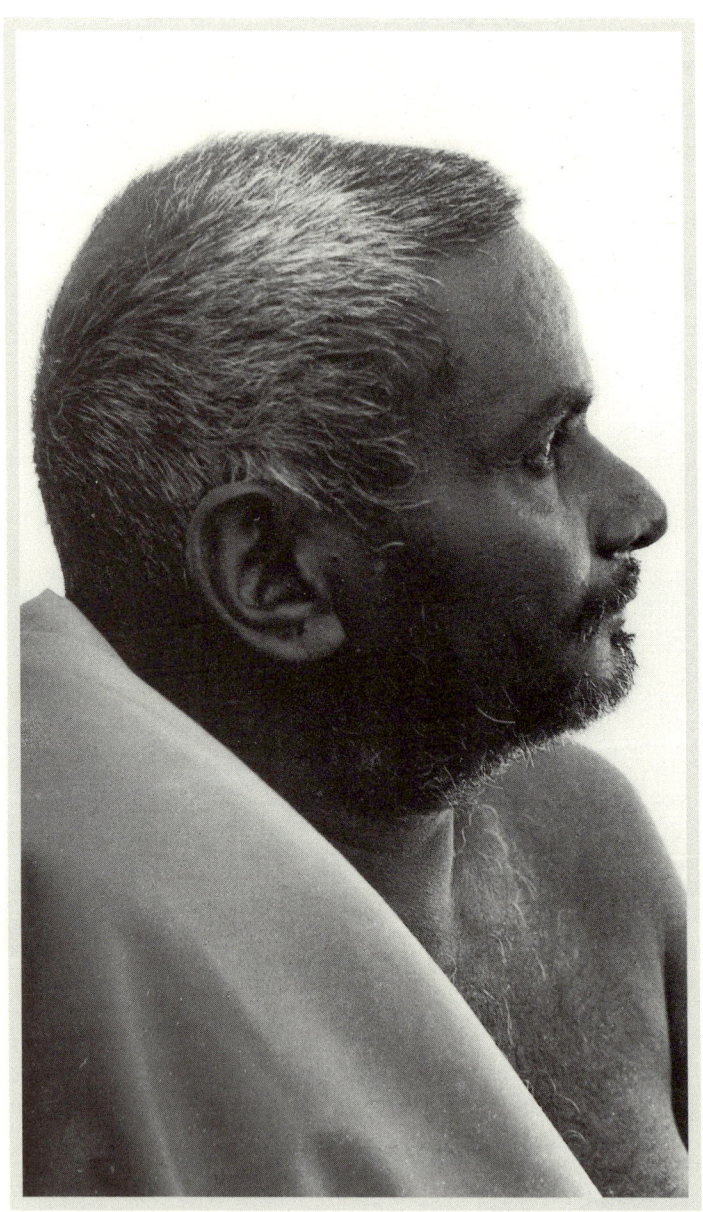

ONE

Remembering the Master

Captain M.U. Hatengdi, retired Naval Secretary at Naval Headquarters in New Delhi, was a long-time disciple of Nityananda. This chapter is his story.

I remember first seeing Nityananda when I was five years old. It was 1920 and he was in the cattle shed of the late Colonel V. R. Miraijkar in Mangalore. Many years later the famous surgeon recounted that on returning home after eight years abroad he had argued with his mother about the young Master to whom she was devoted. He did not understand how a woman so fastidious about cleanliness could tolerate him. This was because in those days the reclusive, rail-thin youth was as likely to be found on a doormat or a dunghill as anywhere. The colonel's mother ordered her son to mind his own business. He regretfully told me that decades passed before he recognized Nityananda's greatness for himself.

In the early 1930s Nityananda still wandered South India and a long time passed before I saw him again. In fact, it was only when I felt an urgent desire for a spiritual teacher that a cousin who visited Ganeshpuri whenever he traveled to Bombay agreed to take me to the ashram. And so it passed that on June 10, 1943, I had my first *darshan* with the Master. The experience evoked in me feelings of reunion with a long-lost friend and an unusual inner peace. I remember not being nervous despite his silence that morning. Later as he stood on the tiny porch outside his room, I boldly asked him three questions. He gave suitable answers although the third concerned mundane matters and his response seemed to imply that I should have known better than to ask it.

After that I saw the Master every Sunday for a while. On one visit a young man ran up to me outside the ashram and asked if he could come. Saying that I thought everyone was welcome, I brought him along. Nityananda was away but we soon saw him approaching from the direction of the river. He seemed to be shouting at the stranger by my side. Entering the ashram, the Master shouted again, asked the startled man who had brought him, and then told him to leave. Turning to me, he said, "Never put yourself out to anyone here. People come with different predilections (*vasanas*) and it's not for you to interfere." My subsequent strict compliance with this directive brought me problems later on—but no matter. I now understood the necessity of keeping to myself and not becoming distracted from my spiritual practice.

On these early visits the Master was often away when I arrived, and it might be an hour before he appeared. I always waited anxiously until I saw him because there were few people about and the ashram felt empty. Unaware of his habitual and sudden disappearances, I thought that perhaps he traveled to Kanhangad periodically and so I asked him. He replied, "I won't go anywhere in the future—only here." As if to avoid further queries he added, "Moreover, traveling these days is difficult." This was during the Second World War when civilians were advised to travel only when necessary. After that Nityananda was always present when I came, either sitting on the cement porch or in his room.

The years from 1944 to 1948 were golden for me. Happily stationed near Bombay, I spent a weekend every month in Ganeshpuri, often alone with the Master. He always greeted me affectionately in Konkani, asking "Have you come?"

Certain other patterns developed during these visits. For instance, he would point to the room I was to occupy, there being only two—one on either side of his own. The peculiarity was that I always stayed in the rooms by turn without deviation. My activities also followed a routine. First I would bathe in the hot springs and then sit to the left of the entrance. Invariably, he always sat on the first step with the narrow doorsill completely blocking my view of him. He never sat facing me. In fact, he would sit for half an hour or more and then walk around only to return to the same spot. This usually went on throughout the waking hours of my visits, which mostly passed in silence. In the beginning, the moment Nityananda sat down near me I would become drowsy and utilize all of my self-control to stay awake. Gradually this experience subsided. I never asked its significance, thinking that sitting near him was simply a form of meditation.

Punctually at ten o'clock every night, he asked me to retire and close the doors. Then, after extinguishing the small kerosene lamp, I lay in total darkness listening to a jungle serenade of frogs and crickets and watching glowworms light the trees with rhythmic regularity. The Master would slowly push open my door at the same time every morning and stand there. And I can't explain how, but my eyes opened every time he stood there in the darkness. As soon as he saw that, he would say, "It's four o'clock," close the door, and walk away. I would rise at once, bathe, and take my place near the entrance. He then joined me for coffee, usually served black and sweetened with *ghee* (clarified butter) because milk was scarce. The affection he showed me was particularly evident when we sat by ourselves after these morning coffee sessions. Such weekends of peace and happiness made me long for his company, and I eagerly awaited the monthly rituals.

Many people have told me that the Master's presence in their lives gave them a tangible sense of security. I know I always felt that he watched over me and an incident from 1946 illustrates this:

> It was dark and the grounds were slippery and treacherous. On my way to the baths, I fell and cut my leg on the sharp stones. In pain and bleeding badly, I washed the wound with rainwater until I thought the bleeding had stopped and then had my bath. Later I was evaluating the injury in my room when Nityananda appeared suddenly, poured a little sandalwood oil on the exact spot, and left as he had come—without a word.

༄

I have stated that our time together mostly passed in silence. However, he did occasionally speak and his words to me at the close of my third visit were particularly significant. "In life," he said, "when a person overcomes one obstacle, another presents itself. This process continues until one's experience is complete and the mind is able to face any situation with the right perspective." To me this was a disheartening idea because I was still young and nursed a number of worldly ambitions. To view life as an obstacle course was not a happy prospect. Still, having sought him out for my spiritual development and not worldly gain, I knew there would be no ultimate disappointment. Already I felt blessed with a strong inner security and a longing for more of his grace.

The Master's conversation could appear casual and years might pass before I appreciated his meaning. For instance, he broke one evening's silence by uttering the solitary sentence that the words of Jesus could also be found in the Bhagavad Gita. This was something about which I was quite ignorant at the time. At other times I discovered that words spoken by him earlier were destined to be fulfilled. Later I heard that when asked how to recognize someone who had attained divine wisdom Nityananda replied that the words of such a person (*jnani*) were always fulfilled.

In 1944 I suffered a tormenting period of inadequacy regarding my spiritual practice. I did not ask him what I should do in fear that he would prescribe some severe breathing exercises or mantra intonation. One night as we sat together I hesitantly asked whether there was a particular book he would advise me to read. His response was instant: "It's not necessary. But if you must, read the Bhagavad Gita."

Nityananda's general disinterest in worldly events never surprised me—but I knew he was aware of them. It was two days after Lord Mountbatten became Viceroy that I arrived at the ashram for my monthly weekend. Sitting near me, the Master said, "While Mountbatten is a good naval officer, he lacks experience in politics." And certainly today an objective historian could substantiate this view.

One Saturday night, with India's independence only four weeks away, Nityananda made some weighty pronouncements about the future. First he asked, "What does *swaraj* mean?" Defining it as "freedom" or "self-rule," he said that India needed additional time to complete its training, hinting that considerable begging and suffering remained for our country. He seemed to say that India's continued dependence on outside assistance would limit our freedom. He added that greedy parties were forcing the situation in the same way that people try to force fruit to ripen before its time. He even predicted our country's division into several states because of petty rivalries and jealousies. And everything he said has come to pass.

I was unable to understand at the time, being overwhelmed like others by the euphoria of India's potential future and greatness. I remember foreigners saying that with so much horsepower we only had to press the accelerator. Alas, today's reality falls short of yesterday's hopes.

Months later, in September 1947, I again heard the Master speak about a great national leader. He said that little time remained for this individual and he wondered whether he was satisfied yet with his fame and accomplishments. Why, Nityananda asked, did he not simply retire from politics, close his eyes, and think of God—for God would come to him, implying that he was a spiritually advanced soul. He added that a person alone, regardless of greatness, cannot do everything. Instead we should each treat life as a relay race, covering the bit of track meant for us as fast as possible before passing on the baton. Four months later, Mahatma Gandhi was assassinated.

On a dark night in June 1945, I was at my usual place by the door to the room nearest the baths. Oddly, Nityananda was sitting behind me some twelve feet away. We were both facing south and peering into the darkness when suddenly he shouted in Konkani, "Who's there?" I had to strain my eyes to see a person slowly moving toward us. "It is I," the man replied. Another shout erupted behind me, "Who?" This question went unheeded, and the stranger approached and put a plate on the step next to me. "What's that?" demanded the Master. This time the man said, *"Satyanarayana prasad."*[1] The Master shouted back: "Prasad for whom?" Repeating this a second time, he added, "Is anything known about this place [meaning himself]?"

I had considered Nityananda to be an incarnate personality since I first received his darshan. This incident only strengthened my belief and I wondered why he seemed angry. Turning to look at him, I saw him in a posture radiating such power that I quickly averted my eyes. With great kindness he said to me, "Prasad means something received with God presenting Himself fully satisfied in the chosen form and bestowing the gift. You may have it now." By offering it to me I knew the prasad had been consecrated. Pointing to the stranger, he then added, "That man did not come for prasad but for *sankalpa*." A sankalpa is a vow taken to perform some action if a prayer is answered, a practice that the Master generally discouraged. As the man began telling his story, my guru admonished him and ordered him to return to the ashram from which he had come.

Several months passed until one evening the Master said: "Mothers are more important—they know what fathers only

---

1. Satyanarayana is a name of Lord Vishnu as well as that of a popular ritual performed to attain certain desired results. Prasad is an offering that has been blessed by a deity or guru.

think to be so. It is the mother who points out the father, brothers, and sisters to the child; this the child believes without question. The mother is to the child what the guru is to the disciple. The guru reveals God to the disciple and enables the disciple to experience His presence."

Sometimes he denied responsibility for his actions— even benevolent ones. One morning in 1946 as we sat in our usual places, a man approached. Nityananda rose, took a stick from the roof, struck him four or five times, replaced the stick, and sat down again. The man left without uttering a sound. Seeing my confusion, the Master said: "This one [referring to himself] has not beaten him. He came to get beaten." And it is indeed true that many people believed such beatings to be blessings that would ward off trouble.

This reminds me of a story about the great Vyasa, author of the *Vedas*, the eighteen *Puranas*, and the *Mahabharata* with its beloved Bhagavad Gita. It is in his honor that we celebrate Guru Purnima every July in India. As he sat one evening on the banks of the river Jumna, some milkmaids carrying pots of curds approached desiring to cross over. Because it was dusk and the river was high, they asked the sage to use his good offices to make the river open a path for them. Vyasa asked them for something to eat, partook of the offered curds, and then addressed the river: "If I have eaten nothing, make a way for these milkmaids." The river complied at once. Because Vyasa always identified with the Absolute (*atman*) and not with his physical body, his true form had not eaten. Nityananda was often described in the same way.

⁌

My visits to Ganeshpuri were infrequent between 1948 to 1954, estranging me from a new generation of devotees.

Then, restationed in Bombay from 1955 to 1957, I often felt lost during my monthly visits. In addition, my few overnights were spent in the big hall since the two rooms flanking Nityananda's room were no longer used by visitors. One was now a kitchen while the other was kept closed and used for storage.

One rainy September night, rather than stay in the big hall I made up my mind to sit outside the kitchen near the Master, who sat there on a bench. At seven o'clock he called to a devotee whom I did not know, asking him to open the closed room for me. I spent the night there surrounded by gifts and other offerings to Nityananda. I departed early the next day, later learning that Nityananda departed the same morning for a new ashram in Kailas.[2]

After 1957, I only visited Ganeshpuri once or twice a year. Because of what I had understood him to mean years earlier, I always kept to myself. Courteous but not overly friendly with other devotees, my behavior had serious consequences. When Nityananda moved his living quarters to the new ashram in Kailas, specific hours were set for darshan. The old ashram's central hall was now usually empty because most devotees gathered in the west hall. On my sporadic visits, I usually occupied a corner of the old hall near the bench where the Master used to sit. My habit was to arrive in the early afternoon and leave by seven the next morning. However, to catch even a glimpse of Nityananda meant knocking hourly at the Kailas doors until they were opened at five o'clock or later. Sometimes special arrangements were made for devotees who had traveled great distances but, a virtual stranger to the new ashram's attendants, I was over-

---

2. The name refers to the mythic Himalayan home of Shiva.

looked. Frustrated, I wondered why the Master failed to make special arrangements for me.

Finally I saw him one evening. He said to me, "Where do you stay these days?" Since he had always seemed to know what I was doing even when stationed to remote areas, I was irked at the question. Petulantly, I replied, "Where else? There." With an admonishing tone, he used his index finger to point to the place I had occupied in the old ashram and said, "Only there is good." I confess that his response was unclear to me at the time. I was too busy thinking that if this were so, why was he in Kailas? But I kept quiet. Only when he left his physical body and his remains were interred near that very spot did I understand.

My last visit before he took *mahasamadhi* was in October 1960. Late in the evening, and after numerous hourly knocks on my part, an attendant opened the door and asked me to sit beside his chair. The Master was resting in his room. About ten minutes passed while two devotees in the passage were trying to work a new tape recorder. The particular words they had managed to catch were of Nityananda repeating, "Without the guru's grace, nothing happens." Thinking of myself, I wondered whether my five-hour wait was due to a lack of grace in my life. What, I fretted, had I done to merit such treatment. As this thought entered my mind, he emerged from his room to lay down again—this time facing me on the adjacent platform. The only light was above my head and he looked directly at me as I nervously shifted my gaze. Nothing was said. Fifteen minutes later, he slowly rose and returned to the platform in his room. I was disturbed by the enormity of his body and wondered how he managed to breathe. My wonder was even greater because I knew how little he ate.

When I informed the attendant of my intended early departure in the morning, he told me to meet him at the baths at four o'clock. I entered the main hall to receive darshan at six. Finding Nityananda asleep on the platform and turned toward the wall, I bent over to see his face. He opened his left eye and nodded to indicate that I could go. Again no words were spoken. Even when my visits became infrequent, he had always said something to me. This was the first and only time that silence reigned. Perhaps he thought I had reached a higher level of understanding—but if so, I was certainly unaware of it. In truth, I left the Master recognizing that a long struggle lay ahead of me. Nevertheless, today as I remember the golden weekends spent in his divine presence, I am filled with inner peace and happiness. I am eternally grateful.

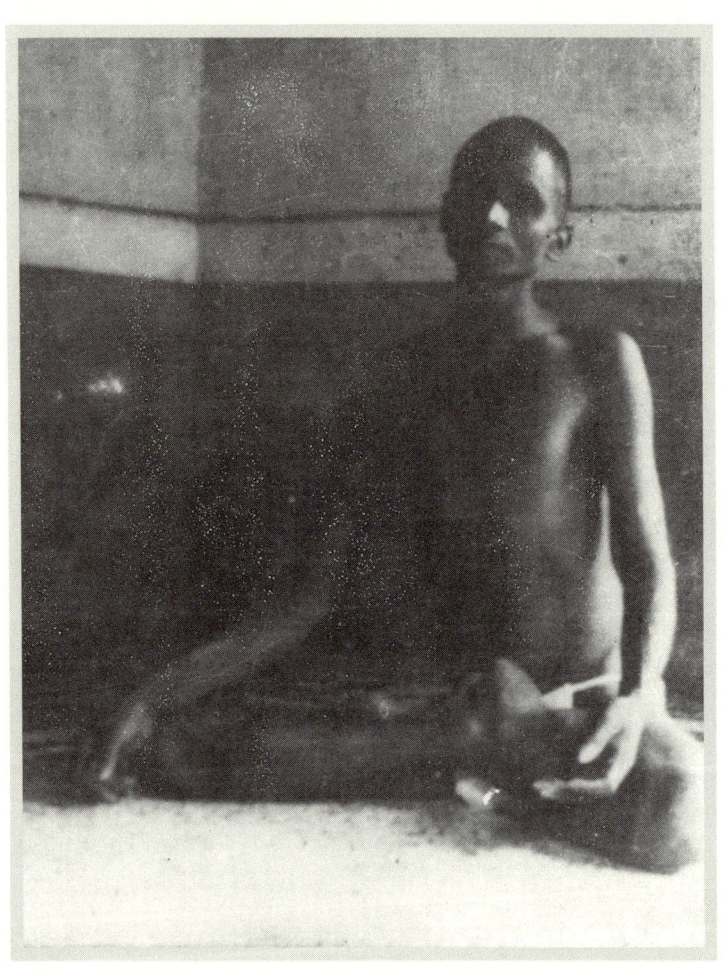

TWO

The Early Years
1900-1915

Nityananda said it didn't matter how or where his human form came into being, that only idle curiosity prompted such useless enquiries. Nevertheless, stories gathered over the years by his devotees present a plausible picture about his birth and boyhood—even though facts often vie for veracity.

At the turn of the century, perhaps late November or early December, light from the setting sun slanted through an area of the dense jungle.[1] On a cashew tree two crows cawed loudly to attract an elderly matriarch of the untouchable caste collecting firewood. Curious, she followed the ruckus—and under a bush discovered a baby boy with skin the color of ripe wheat carefully wrapped in a white cloth. Now, the old woman already had a large family but remembered that Unniamma's mother wanted to adopt a child for her barren daughter. So she dutifully picked up the infant and took him home.

---

1. Called Guruvana, it is a few miles from the Kanhangad Rock ashram. Later it will be the second temple dedicated to Nityananda, inaugurated in May 1966 by Mr. Silam, then lieutenant governor of Pondicherry.

The following morning she proceeded straight to the village of Unniamma's mother, who accepted the baby with great joy. To seal the bargain, Unniamma's mother gave the old woman ten pounds of rice and then hurried to Pantalayini near Calicut, in an area known as Koilande. There her daughter worked in the neighboring temples as well as in the household of Ishwar Iyer, a respected lawyer. Unniamma gratefully adopted the baby and named him Ram.

At about eighteen months of age, Ram developed liver troubles. And even though Mr. Iyer hired for him the best ayurvedic practitioner, the baby's condition worsened. He grew thin and his stomach became distended. Because he often cried through the night, Unniamma's landlord finally demanded that she get rid of him. Too agitated to go to work the next day, she instead took her ailing son out for some fresh air. As she walked, she suddenly saw a tall dark-skinned stranger carrying a large satchel. The distraught mother, thinking he was a physician, approached and begged him to help her child. As if expecting her, he removed a packet from his bag and instructed her to mix its contents with the flesh of a freshly killed crow fried in clarified butter (ghee). She should then administer a small dose to Ram each morning before he had eaten. Also, she should rub Ram's skin with the crow's blood. At this very moment, a toddy tapper [2] walked by and handed her the crow he carried in his right hand. Astonished, she looked up to thank the two men—but they had vanished.

Unniamma started the prescribed treatment at once, and the child recovered in a short time. The crow's blood, however, permanently turned his skin a dark blue hue. Years later

---

2. Sap from the toddy palm is collected by toddy tappers for making a fermented beverage called arrack.

when questioned about any aspect of his background, Nityananda often quipped that a crow came and a crow left. He also said that his skin was not black but blue-black (*Krishnavarna*).

A devout man, Mr. Iyer worshipped the Sun deity Bharga—and he loved Ram, for whom he felt a strong mystical attraction. When Unniamma died, the kindly man brought the six-year-old into his household and proceeded to take him everywhere. This included the famous Krishna temple at Guruvayur where, alone together, Ram revealed an esoteric understanding that both astounded the older man and satisfied his spiritual hunger. A famous astrologer told him the child was an incarnate personality and that he was blessed to have him as ward and companion. This caused talk among colleagues and friends who were shocked to see the respected Brahmin's attachment to the lower caste boy.

The young Ram was mischievous and loved to pull pranks, and his foster father asked friends and servants to keep an eye on him. For instance, he would dive into a neighboring temple's water tank, stay under water for a long time, and then run off dripping water everywhere. He would also get up by four in the morning and insist that other household members do likewise, taking their baths and applying sacred ash to their foreheads. He refused to attend school but agreed to learn subjects like Malayalam, English, Sanskrit, and arithmetic from Mr. Iyer.

One story tells of Ram tricking a local snake-charmer who ran a dishonest money-making operation. Under cover of darkness his cohorts would release several cobras into the compound of a selected household. The snake-charmer would then appear the following morning to offer his assistance. Calling the snakes, he would depart with both the reptiles and his fee. However, trying the scheme one day on Mr. Iyer—the snakes would not heed their call. The baffled snake-charmer soon noticed Ram in the background giggling. He had rendered the trickster's mantra ineffective. The boy then let him collect his snakes with the warning never to bother the Iyer household again.

When Ram was around ten years old, Mr. Iyer decided to take him on a pilgrimage to the city of Benares and other holy places. As usual the two traveled alone together. On this trip the boy reportedly granted to his companion many divine visions. Along the way Ram took leave of his tearful foster father, promising to see him again. Exactly where the young Master went, nobody knows. However, it is thought that he traveled the northern regions, for some sources indicate his renown in the Himalayas as a great kundalini yogi. Six years later Ram returned. Having had the boy in his thoughts for days and realizing that he had really come home, Mr. Iyer ecstatically repeated *nityananda, nityananda!* Eternal bliss! And this, of course, became the Master's popular name.

Shortly thereafter Mr. Iyer performed his youngest daughter's marriage ceremony at the temple in Guruvayur. There, the entire family felt the deity's presence in Nityananda. The youth then took his foster father to receive the darshan of Ananteshwar and Lord Krishna in Udipi. (Later Nityananda would indicate to devotees his previous association with the ancient Ananteshwar temple by remarking that he had been present when it was built some 400 years earlier.) Mr. Iyer soon fell gravely ill and, resting in Nityananda's lap, asked to see Bharga, the divine object of his lifelong worship. The young Master granted his wish and

Mr. Iyer died. To express his love and gratitude before he died, the man bequeathed some assets to his adopted son. The young Nityananda refused the gift.

THREE

South Kanara
1915-1936

After performing last rites for his foster father, the young Nityananda took off again, this time to wander South India and beyond. Over the years devotees heard him mention stowing away on a cargo ship, probably boarding in Madras, to work as a stoker boy and sailing to Ceylon, Rangoon, and Singapore. He spoke of being a laborer on a Burmese rubber plantation and some people think he visited Japan.

He once laughingly recounted an incident during the First World War when, as an army conscript, he was declared medically unfit because the doctor could not find his heartbeat or pulse. He is said to have been in Madras when Swami Vivekananda left India in 1896 and again when he died in 1902. In the mid-1950s, when asked if he would travel abroad like certain other Indian swamis, he answered, "One only has to go if unable to see places or deal with people from here."

The following is one of the few authenticated stories from this time period. The scene is Palani Temple where Lord Subramanya, a brother of Lord Ganesh in Hindu mythology, is the presiding deity. We must visualize Nityananda in those days looking like an eccentric wanderer, his wire-thin body healthy and glowing. Late one morning he was ascending the last few steps to the shrine when the attendant priest, having just locked the doors after morning worship, was descending. Nityananda asked him to re-open the doors and wave a ritual light and incense (*arati*) before the deity. Astonished that a vagrant would dare make such a request, the priest curtly told Nityananda that the time for morning worship was over.

Nityananda continued on. The priest, expecting him to walk around the shrine and worship at the Muslim altar in the back, was not concerned until he heard the temple bells ringing. Turning, he was astonished to see the doors open, Nityananda sitting in the deity's place, and arati being waved before him by invisible hands. The vision vanished at once and Nityananda left the shrine to stand on one leg for some time, steadily gazing upward. Coins poured at his feet, offered, some say, by pilgrims, while others say by an unseen source. In any case, he was accorded all the honors of a Master. When the surrounding pilgrims begged him to stay, he refused and instructed them to use the money to provide a daily meal of rice porridge to visiting renunciates. It was later learned that local *sanyasis* had been praying for this very thing.

Leaving the Pantalayani area, the young Master encountered an errant gang of youths in Cannanore. One of them wrapped a kerosene-soaked rag on the Master's left hand and set it ablaze. Nityananda didn't resist physically but instead transferred the burning sensation to the one who had attacked him. Crying out in pain, the unexpected victim begged for mercy. As Nityananda extinguished the fire on his own hand, the sensation in the other's subsided. Years later, he explained to devotees:

> Those with inner wisdom (jnanis) do not go in for miracles. However, this does not mean that a burning rag tied to their hands does not hurt. They suffer like anyone else but have the capacity to detach their minds completely from the nerve centers. In this way they might remember the pain only once or twice a day.

※

At some point the young Nityananda began appearing regularly around Mangalore and other parts of South Kanara. Again, extant stories make a clear chronology impossible.

Now approaching his early twenties and wearing only a loincloth and often not even that, he lived a life of great simplicity in the region's rocks, caves, and forests. It was a familiar sight to see him standing stiffly in a tree before the local Mahakali temple at Kaup. People would gather below his tree, mingling without regard for caste or creed, and the Master would shower them with leaves that recipients prized for their healing power. One day, after the crowd dispersed, a blind man stayed behind and begged for help, explaining the burden he was to his family. After a while, saying nothing, Nityananda climbed down and rubbed the man's eyes with leaves from the tree. The man arose next morning to find his sight restored.

Another time, in Manjeshwar, there was a man whose mother suffered from a painful lump in her leg. When medicines brought no relief, he went to Nityananda, who was standing as usual in a tree. He said, "This one knows and is there." The son, however, did not understand. He went home and returned with his mother in a carriage—but the

Master had vanished. After searching in vain, they went home to find him descending from their attic. He silently massaged the astonished woman's leg for several minutes and then departed. The mother recovered completely.

Yet another story tells of a widow who brought her six-year-old daughter. Nityananda said, "But the child has been blind from birth. Why do you insist I change this? Let the child say what she wants." The child then said, "I would like to see my mother once." The Master said nothing. After a while he asked them to leave. It was the mother's custom to first bathe the child, put her in a safe spot, and then perform her own ablutions. That day, as she returned, her daughter jumped up and shouted that she saw her. Their joy lasted only minutes before the blindness returned. It seems Nityananda chose not to interfere with the child's destiny.

※

One morning on a busy road near a village that some say was Panambur, the Master strode along at his usual rapid pace. Coming upon a pregnant woman, he stopped suddenly and squeezed her breasts. The woman did not resist but when outraged people began rushing toward him, Nityananda continued walking. He quickly outdistanced them, shouting that this time the child would live. The woman hurriedly told onlookers that her three previous children had died after their first breast feeding. Shortly thereafter, her baby was born and survived. A village delegation was organized to thank him and the story spread.

This time Nityananda's unconventional behavior became clarified after the fact, but it was not always the case. For example, prior to 1920 he was often seen in the early morning hours waiting for a cow to pass. Following it, he would catch the droppings and swallow them before they touched the ground. Another story says he came to the flooded Pavanje River during the monsoon season. When the boatman refused to ferry him, the Master simply walked across. When in 1953 someone asked him to explain the river incident, he said:

> True, the Pavanje River was in flood when this one walked across and the boatman would not venture out. But there was no motive—it was just the mood of the moment. The only meaning was that the boatman was deprived of his half *anna*.
>
> One must live in the world like common men. Once established in infinite consciousness, one becomes silent and, knowing all, goes about as if knowing nothing. Although he may be doing many things in several places, he outwardly appears as if he is simply a witness of life—like a spectator at the cinema. He is unaffected by events, whether pleasant or unpleasant. The ability to forget everything and remain detached is the highest state possible.

∽

Nityananda was indifferent to social conventions, often going naked in the early days. When some people objected and reported the matter, he was taken before a local magistrate. As always, a crowd followed. When ordered to wear a loincloth, the Master reportedly replied, "To cover which with what?" The magistrate then instructed a policeman to tie a loincloth around him—but it wouldn't stay tied. Finally, in exasperation the magistrate ordered a tailor to secure it with needle and thread. The tailor was also a devotee and pleaded with Nityananda to let it stay in place. He complied, it remained, and thereafter a loincloth was his usual article of clothing.

Nityananda passed most of the time around 1915 on the beach at Kanhangad, lying on the hot sand and gazing at the sun. A devotee who as a boy often accompanied his father to the town said, years later, that it was impossible to approach Nityananda in the afternoons. The intense heat discouraged everybody from walking on the sand. Sometimes he sat from morning until evening on the blazing hot rock where his first temple would be built in 1963.

FOUR

Discovery in Udipi
1918

By 1918, the tiny village of Udipi was already a well-known center of pilgrimage. Here people could visit the Krishna temple, the birthplace of the third great teacher Madhvacharya, the ancient Ananteshwar temple, and the area called Ajjara Kadu (or "Grandfathers' Wood").

Two friends strolled together here every evening, always ending their walk by circling the two temples.[1] Once, passing the Krishna temple, they were drawn to a thin young man who stood among the sanyasis in the outer corridor. At that moment the youth turned to face the wall and refused to be acknowledged. The friends both agreed that this was an uncommon holy man. Several days later they came upon him, this time at an entrance to the temple. Seeing them, Nityananda began to laugh uncontrollably. He did so for a prolonged period, and in a way that Mr. Bhat later said seemed to come from the depths of his being.

---

1. In 1966 Captain Hatengdi contacted Mr. K. Shivanna Bhat in Bombay for this version of how he and his friend the late Dr. R. Kombarbail met Nityananda. His friend later became a Bombay physician revered for treating his poor patients for free.

Weeks passed before they saw him again, this time sitting by himself outside the ancient Ananteshwar temple. Dr. Kombarbail caught hold of both his hands and asked him who he was and where he came from. He addressed him in Hindi, Kanarese, and English in quick succession. Nityananda had apparently been observing silence for some time because it took great effort for him to speak—but he did so in fluent English, Hindi, and Konkani, which was the local language. He ended by repeating, *"Nityananda, nityananda!"* The two men realized he referred to his blissful state and this is why devotees from those early days called him "Sadhu" or "Swami."

Mr. Bhat, having performed his father's anniversary ceremony that morning, invited the sadhu to his house for a special meal. To his delight, the Master readily accepted and ate his food from a plantain leaf and discarded the leaf himself. This was the last time he was observed to eat with his own hands. Subsequently, he ate only when fed by devotees. Even water he allowed devotees to pour into his mouth, indicating after a few swallows that he was satisfied.

Nityananda stayed in Udipi for a time, often visiting Mangalore and Kaup, but he stayed nowhere for long. Mrs. T. Sitabai, Captain Hatengdi's primary source concerning these days, felt the young Master was pulled mystically by devotees thinking of him or experiencing some stress. She said Nityananda would often leave Udipi abruptly without indicating his destination and then reappear some time later. For instance, one afternoon at half past three, he suddenly stood up and said he would return soon. And in fact, by five o'clock he was back. No one inquired nor did he indicate where he had been. Two days later a devotee arrived from Mangalore to say how in the early afternoon of that particular day his fellow devotees were longing to see him. Within minutes, he appeared. As on other occasions, no one asked how he covered the fifty-odd miles to the seaport town. They were content knowing that, when needed, Nityananda often came.

Mrs. Krishnabai, an early devotee, describes a similar incident. It was to be Nityananda's first visit to her house in Mangalore—but when he arrived, he immediately turned and walked away with his usual speed. A crowd watched as Mrs. Krishnabai's husband and a friend tried to stop him physically. However, the sadhu easily swept both men along with him for a quarter mile before suddenly saying "She stopped me," and agreeing to return. It seemed that Mrs. Krishnabai's anguish was too great for him to ignore.

∽

In the beginning, to keep him from the Krishna temple, street urchins in Udipi pelted the young Nityananda with stones. Oddly, those finding their mark were transformed into jewels (or sweets, according to similar stories from Kanhangad). But those who scrambled to retrieve such treasures found only stones. When, after several days of this phenomenon, a pile of stones appeared at the feet of Krishna's temple statue, the matter was reported to the elderly swami in charge. Recognizing that Nityananda was no ordinary sadhu, he at once ordered everyone to treat him with respect.

Throughout his life, Nityananda was a friend of beggars, the lowest castes, and the poor. He would let the money left at his feet by devotees accumulate and then order a feast for the poor, insisting on the best ingredients. Even when resources were scarce, food was still miraculously abundant. This became a regular event wherever he wandered, and in later years he only accepted invitations from hosts willing to feed the needy. The Master himself liked to dish up regional specialties for his guests with his two huge hands—like Mangalore's *iddlies* cooked in jackfruit leaves. To this day in Ganeshpuri, feeding the local poor children (known as *Bal Bhojan* in India) still occurs in Nityananda's name.

Among those who sought his company in Udipi was a wealthy landlord's only son. The father, however, considered the Master to be a dangerous eccentric and became alarmed when the schoolboy began giving money to help feed the poor. He decided to hire two assassins to kill Nityananda, a practice not uncommon for people of means in those days. In this instance, because of his intended victim's frequent disappearances, the father thought the abduction would go unnoticed.

One afternoon, while sitting on a veranda, the Master suddenly smiled, stood up, and disappeared down the lane. His devotees quickly followed—and found him held by one man and about to be stabbed by another. They overpowered the assassins, attracted the police, and only then noticed that the man who had wielded the knife was in excruciating pain, his arm frozen in its attack position. At Nityananda's touch, the man's arm dropped painlessly to his side.

As the assailants were taken to jail, the protesting Nityananda followed and requested their release. The police refused. He then sat down and remained there for three days without food or water while his devotees negotiated with officials. Eventually, the prisoners were released. It is said that they became devotees of the Master and that even the local officials developed a high regard for the eccentric sadhu.

᪲

Late one night, a devotee was told by alarmed women of his

household that Nityananda was running a high temperature. However, the sadhu refused to leave his refuge, the filthy cattle shed, repeating, "The medicine is here." Thinking him delirious, the host pleaded with his guest until he finally agreed to move to the veranda.

Hurrying to the only chemist in Udipi, the devotee returned with a bottle of reddish-brown mixture for his fever. Nityananda shook the bottle, handed it back, and said, "What is this? Look at it." Removing the cork, the devotee found to his consternation that the liquid had changed color and now smelled like cow urine. The Master laughed and said it was no better than what was in the cattle shed.

This was the monsoon season when people customarily collected rainwater in drums placed below the eaves of their houses. The night of his fever, Nityananda suddenly began to gulp down the rainwater in his host's drum. Witnesses could not believe the amount of water he drank. When he finished, he turned and said, "The fever is gone." And it was.

※

Indian families used to perform a special ceremony six days after a birth to honor the goddess of destiny, who was thought to write the newborn's future that night. On one occasion, and six days after a devotee's wife had given birth, Nityananda entered her room, swallowed the dried umbilical cord, and left. When questioned about his behavior, he replied that this particular family had lost many children in infancy but that the new baby would survive.

※

Sometimes Nityananda humorously acted out a charade to describe an upcoming visitor. One morning he slung an empty shopping bag over his left shoulder, bending slightly from the weight; in his right hand he pretended to carry something light. He then walked up and down the room before suddenly taking off for a neighbor's house. Following, perplexed devotees saw a man pacing the street looking for someone. He carried a heavy bag on his left shoulder and a water container in his right hand. By now the Master was sitting on his neighbor's veranda. Approaching the steps, the stranger stopped and they gazed silently at one another for a long time. Finally the Master stood up and the man walked away.

The man remained in the area for a while. When devotees asked him about the encounter, he described himself as a Krishna devotee from Uttar Pradesh. Having had a vision that Krishna was present in living form in Udipi, he traveled to the village, where he felt drawn vibrationally to that particular neighborhood. Unsure of the exact house, he had wandered around for some time before Nityananda appeared. He added, "I said nothing to him because with one look I knew why I was there. Tomorrow I will leave blissfully happy having received darshan of Krishna."

Wistfully, Mrs. Sitabai related an event that happened when she was both a new devotee and newly married. One day Nityananda picked up a coconut and offered it to her. Now, it is rare and auspicious to receive a coconut from a holy person. Moreover, it is thought to keep widowhood at bay, and a married woman would traditionally extend the skirt of her sari with both hands to receive it. But the young Mrs. Sitabai hesitated. She considered her high-caste birth and whether it was acceptable for her to receive such a thing from a casteless sadhu. He waited patiently for several minutes and when she did not accept the offering, he threw it away—perhaps deciding that her fate held too strong a pull on her. Three months later, her husband died. And she would always wonder whether she might have been spared widowhood had her faith been stronger.

⁂

In the early twenties, Nityananda frequently visited Mrs. Krishnabai's Mangalore residence, which included several small rental houses. In those days residents used a row of simple lavatories situated at the edge of the compound. Each morning municipal workers would arrive with a cart to collect the night soil and take it away.

We know that Nityananda's eating habits were as unpredictable as his movements. Only partaking of food and water that was fed to him, he would appear unexpectedly at Mrs. Krishnabai's door looking hopeful. Sometimes the family had already eaten and there might only be a few morsels of rice to put in his mouth. But this always seemed to satisfy him.

One morning, however, compound residents were horrified to see the Master by the lavatories sitting among piles of night soil. Always an early riser, he appeared to have collected the matter with his own hands and formed the mounds, covering himself from head to toe in the process. He held a bamboo scale in his hand and when anyone passed, he said, "Bombay *halwa*[2]. Very tasty! Would you like some?" Then he would raise the scale as if to weigh out the desired quantity. He sat there all day, embarrassing everyone, even taking his afternoon nap there. When Mrs. Krishnabai finally approached, he said, "You feed me, don't you? But would you also feed me this?" Abashed, she turned away.

---

2. An Indian sweet confection

That evening Mrs. Krishnabai was afraid he would drop by the house without washing. She asked two of the assembled devotees to wait at the door to prevent him from bringing the filth inside. And promptly at seven o'clock, he appeared at the back door. In those days he could be prevailed upon, at least in some matters, and the two devotees ended up taking him to the baths for a thorough scrubbing. Later, sitting with his devotees, Nityananda held out his palm and asked if they could smell the "fine Parisian perfume." He never explained the meaning of the day's events—and they never asked.

The next morning Mrs. Krishnabai found all the compound's residents lined up before the Master asking his pardon. Drawing one of them aside, she inquired what had happened. The man explained: Earlier that week while discussing how Nityananda only ate food fed to him, someone had joked about offering him night soil. He went on, "We now realize how wrong we were and that such a Master can find nourishment in anything—even filth. Therefore we seek his forgiveness."

FIVE

The Mangalore Days of Rail Travel
1923-1933

Nityananda loved trains. He traveled frequently by rail and even established his Kanhangad ashram beside the tracks in 1925. When he was in Mangalore he would settle into one of the empty boxcars shunted aside at the station, and here devotees could find him.

One afternoon Mrs. Krishnabai, learning of his arrival, hurried off to receive darshan. She quickly returned home to greet a relative who had come for a visit. A sanyasi, he asked her to take him to see Nityananda the next day. Later, as they stepped down from the boxcar, Mrs. Krishnabai turned to the Master and said, "I came yesterday in such a hurry, never dreaming that I would also be able to return today." But Nityananda replied, "Who are you to decide?"

He often rode the trains between Mangalore and Kanhangad. Once a railroad official who was new to the route ordered him to disembark for not having a ticket. As he made no sign to obey, the official forcibly removed him at Manjeshwar. Submitting to the rough handling, Nityananda proceeded to make himself comfortable on a station bench. But when its departure time came—the train didn't move. Minutes ticked by and people waited expectantly. Finally, some passengers told the official that it was unwise to treat this particular sadhu so harshly. Devotees then took Nityananda on board and the train began moving. When it reached Kanhangad, however, it went past the station and stopped where his ashram currently stands. The Master descended wearing around his neck a garland made of hundreds of tickets. He handed the garland to the same official, asking him to take as many as he wanted. Shamefaced, the man said it would not happen again. Nityananda then jumped the small ditch and strode off toward the jungle. Again the train would not move, and devotees ran after him for help. He retraced his steps, slapped the engine, and told it to get going. And the train did, going in reverse back to the station it had bypassed earlier.

Probably due to such incidents, Nityananda had free run of the trains. Engineers welcomed him into their engine cars and even blew a saluting whistle when passing his ashram, a custom still followed today. It is said that throughout the late 1920s the Master always had a punched ticket attached to the string of his loincloth.

Swami Chidananda of Rishikesh recalled that, as a child traveling south by train from Mangalore, he once noticed a commotion at a wayside station. Peering out the window, he watched a reed-thin Nityananda toss biscuits and sweets from a vendor's tray to a crowd of delighted children. Then, giving the pleased vendor a currency note from his loincloth, he climbed into the engine car as the departing whistle blew.

Udipi residents watched him catch cow droppings to put on his head. Then, whistling like a locomotive, he would chug away down the road like a child.

And he used a railroad analogy in his last public talk. This was on Guru Purnima, July 27, 1961, twelve days before his passing. He addressed the assembled devotees at some length, talking about the energy required to pull a train up a hill and of a spiritual seeker's need to stay firmly on the proverbial tracks.

Nityananda traveled constantly between Mangalore, Kanhangad, Udipi, Akroli and other villages. His appearances, generally unexpected, seemed magical. One day, thinking him in Mangalore, six or seven Udipi devotees decided to pay a social call on a neighboring village. Approaching a wooded area along the way, they were astonished to see the Master sitting under a tree. The devotees immediately changed their plans and decided to spend the evening there with him. When Nityananda shouted at them to keep their distance, they sat down some twenty feet away. They could hear him talking and, as their eyes adjusted to the gloom, they saw a cobra coiled at his side. It was to the snake that the Master spoke in Konkani, and it seemed to nod in the affirmative. The only words the devotees could clearly distinguish were, "Are you three comfortable?" and they inferred that there were two other snakes nearby. After a while, Nityananda patted the cobra on its hood and watched it disappear.

∽

As witnessed, Nityananda's behavior could be difficult to interpret. While a person might think that he or she had been forced to undergo a minor difficulty, later reflection would indicate that something more serious had been miraculously averted. Many devotees experienced this as we see in the following story.

The young Master often visited the home of a devoted Mangalore woman. Once he told her married daughter, "She is this one's mother; yours is here," indicating himself. One evening Nityananda walked into the kitchen as the devotee was cooking over the mud hearth. He pulled out a burning piece of firewood, hit her over the head with it, and quickly left. Her children were outraged but the mother advised patience, and an explanation was neither sought nor provided. Twelve months later, while casting the family's horoscopes, an astrologer from Kerala expressed his astonishment at finding the lady of the house alive. He said his calculations showed that she should have died the previous year. That was when her family realized that the Master's blow had changed his devotee's destiny.

༄

Mrs. Lakshmibai was a young, widowed domestic in the employ of Tulsiamma, a well-known devotee. The young servant was devoted to Nityananda as well. One day she was asked to prepare the evening meal early because Tulsiamma hoped to bring Nityananda home to dinner. Now, Mrs. Lakshmibai had always nursed an intense desire to feed him with her own hands, having watched other devotees do so. Overcoming her shyness, she asked if she might accompany her mistress in case the Master refused their offer. But like Cinderella, she was told to stay home and make the house ready. So saying, Tulsiamma left.

Finishing her preparations, Mrs. Lakshmibai went outside to gather fresh plantain leaves for serving the food. Still musing over her disappointment, she slowly cut a leaf and heard an unexpected rustle in the tree above. Nityananda climbed down, asked if the meal was ready, and preceded her to the house. The overjoyed servant ran to wash her hands and began to feed the Master. At that moment Tulsiamma returned. Her words "I couldn't find him" were rapidly followed by her amazed laughter at finding the Master already enjoying dinner at her house.

※

Appayya Alva was a prosperous South Kanara landlord renowned and sometimes feared for his ability to materialize objects through the strength of mantra. This powerful mantravadi, with a wave of his hands, could produce foreign cigarettes, exotic fruits, or flowers by the armful. However, when they materialized in one place, they disappeared elsewhere—often from the Car Street flower market in Mangalore where attendants would suddenly wail, "My flowers are gone!" And so it was that many people suffered from his exhibitions. Alva was also a vain and arrogant man. One time, when his presence at a concert went unrecognized, he caused the singer to temporarily lose his voice.

Eventually Alva encountered Nityananda. One May day in 1923 Mr. M. A. K. Rao, an esteemed Manjeshwar citizen, was celebrating a niece's wedding. At Mr. Rao's insistence, Nityananda was invited and seated in a place of honor. It was while the soon-to-marry couple placed garlands around the Master's neck that Alva made his entrance. He immediately belittled the host for honoring the young sadhu as if he were a divine being and boasted that he would prove his point. Reciting a mantra, he then rolled a tobacco leaf between his hands and forced it into the Master's mouth.

Nityananda chewed and swallowed the leaf as if it had been offered by a devotee. As people watched, he perspired slightly—but Alva suddenly sank to the ground mortally ill. He died three days later in the Government Wenlock Hospital.

Twenty years later Nityananda was asked about this incident. He played down the connection between the tobacco leaf and Alva's death, saying that the man had misused his considerable mantric powers to bring suffering to the poor and misery to the weak. He said that divine forces had stopped the abuse and he called the tobacco leaf insignificant. He then revealed that, before dying, Alva asked to see Nityananda but his family refused to send for him.

In 1923, at the height of the monsoon season, Nityananda walked through the marketplace in Bantwal. By this time he was a known figure in the district, recognized by devotees and skeptics alike. As it was raining heavily, he entered a shop and stood in the corner with the servants and porters. The shopkeepers ordered him to leave, taunting him about his great powers. When Nityananda asked to stay, they laughed and splashed him with water. Only then did he walk away, sadly saying, "It seems God has decided that only Mother Ganga* can wash away the sins here." The shopkeepers retorted, "Let her come. That way we can perform our ablutions without going to her banks!"

Even as they spoke, the swollen Netravati River rumbled and began to swallow the village. It was one of the worst floods in South Kanara, and Bantwal was destroyed. A span of the Ullal railroad bridge was damaged so badly that train

---

* the Ganges River

service was disrupted for months. People still talk about Nityananda pulling many poor victims from the swirling waters.

~

Perhaps the most extraordinary incident of this period occurred in a devotee's house in Falnir just before sunset. While they sat before him in meditation, those present were suddenly disturbed by a blinding flash of light on the wall behind Nityananda. They opened their eyes to find him motionless on his knees in a yoga posture (*veera-padmasana*) with his eyes closed. Afraid to touch him, they lit lamps and tried to see if he still breathed. Finding no signs of life, they decided that he had taken mahasamadhi and invited people to come for their last darshan. Most devotees soon returned to their homes, some sad and disappointed that the young sadhu had left them, some hopeful that he would return, and some thinking that he had overdone his breathing exercise.

Mrs. Krishnabai was one of the few who stayed behind, maintaining a vigil throughout the night and following day. That afternoon Nityananda suddenly moved. He stretched his limbs and was immediately helped to a bed. He wore a strange look and recognized no one for quite some time. After questioning, he admitted that he had gone for good—but five divine beings persuaded him to return, saying that it was too soon. During his remaining years, the Master never spoke of it again.

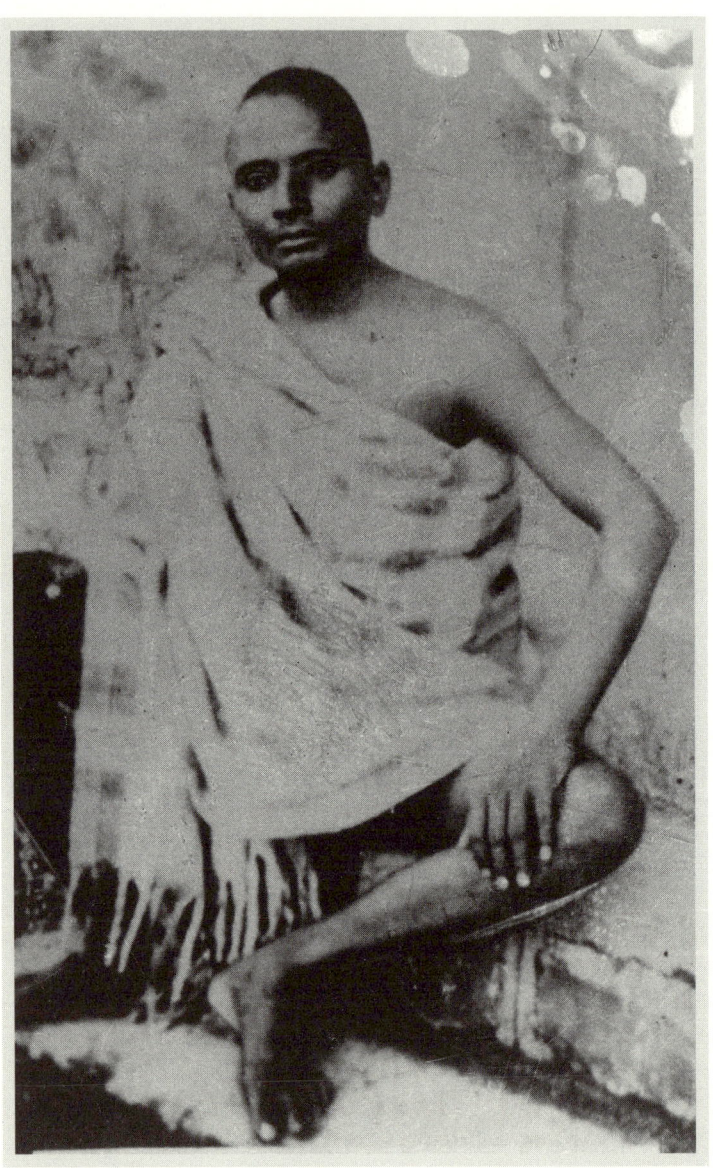

SIX

Kanhangad's Rock Ashram
1925-1936

Before leaving South Kanara, around 1925 Nityananda began spending long periods in Kanhangad. Initially he chose the jungle area called Guruvana for his rock ashram.* Evidence indicates that he inhabited a certain jungle cave where he had discovered a skeleton seated in a lotus position, surrounded by pots and other personal effects. Nityananda is said to have disposed of it in an unknown manner. This story came from an elderly woman in Kerala who fed Nityananda during this time. She also said that at the rear of the cave was once an entrance, now blocked off, to a hall that could seat several hundred people. Nityananda often said that beyond the hill in Guruvana were many saints in samadhi. Some people believe he was associated with this particular spot in a previous incarnation and the skeleton was either his own or of someone he knew.

Regardless, it was here that Nityananda struck a rock from which spring water has flowed ever since. Nearby he

---

* Devotees believe Nityananda was found abandoned here as an infant. Guruvana lies several miles from a second temple that was dedicated to Nityananda in 1966.

placed eight stone balls thought to represent the occult powers achieved through yogic discipline (*siddhis*) and a tank to collect the spring water. When B. H. Mehta built the temple in 1966 he added a spout, called Papanashini Ganga, for the water to pass through. For many years Swami Janananda tended the area, converting the jungle into a spiritual paradise. He rebuilt the tank as a well, constructed a road to the temple, and replaced the stone balls with eight stone linga-like structures. He also made a small shrine for Malbir, the area's protecting spirit.

Nityananda's work on the Kanhangad fort started around 1927. First he built a road, still used, from the travelers' bungalow up to the rock temple and ashram. He then began clearing the jungle growth that overran the dilapidated compound. Historically the site belonged to a long lineage of chieftains. At one time it was in the hands of the Tulu dynasty who ruled from Mangalore to Kanhangad. Nityananda began the project to the consternation of local authorities who pestered him with questions about his activities and whether he had permission. The Master always responded that he was clearing the jungle for their future offices, a prediction that eventually came to pass.

Once the fort was cleared of overgrowth, Nityananda turned his attention to the rock itself, which is where the temple erected to him in 1963 now stands. He wanted caves hewn from the rock and, without engineers or blueprints, directed everything down to the most minute detail. The task was formidable. Using no equipment, workers carved out the caves by hand. Within three years some forty caves stood ready, properly cemented and plastered inside and out. Most were large enough for a person to sit and rest. There were six entrances; three faced east and three faced west, resulting in continuous light in the passages from sunrise to sunset.

With work proceeding on the interior of the compound, Nityananda often worked on the exterior. He made the steps and lingas with his own hands. Following a visit to the caves in 1945, Captain Hatengdi asked him about their symbolism. He replied that they represented the brain and its six passages. At one point a well was dug within the cave complex, but Nityananda later ordered it closed. Today an outside well is the current ashram's main water source.

Local laborers received their pay at the end of each day. Swami Janananda recalled that the foreman usually collected the money from beneath a tree. But sometimes the workers filed past Nityananda. Opening and then closing his empty fist, he would drop the exact wages into each recipient's hand.

One day a delegation of local authorities arrived and asked him about the source of these wages. Without a word, Nityananda led them to the waterlogged field beside the rock, dived in, and emerged with a bagful of currency. He told the astonished men that a crocodile in the depths always supplied the amount he needed. He then added that they were free to find it themselves; otherwise he offered to bring up the beast for them to see.

Feeling that they had been ridiculed by this yogi in a loincloth, the angry delegates immediately reported the unauthorized construction. They told Mr. Gawne, the British tax official in South Kanara, that a crazy sanyasi was paying workers with money from unknown and mysterious sources. It seemed that Mr. Gawne had heard of Nityananda's remarkable activities in Mangalore and decided to see for himself. Arriving at the Kanhangad railway station, he proceeded on horseback accompanied by his dog along the road built by the Master. Reaching the rock compound, he stopped and looked around. Nityananda was in a cave below the ruins on the fort's south side. Here, the dog soon discovered him and started to bark.

He emerged from the cave and Mr. Gawne, still on horseback, asked him why he was doing all this work and for whom. Nityananda replied in English, "Not for this one [meaning himself]. If you want it, you may have it." As the words were uttered, a change came over the British official. Turning, he ordered the local authorities to leave Nityananda alone and allow him free rein of the site. He added that the source of funds was of no concern as long as no one complained of being swindled or robbed. Imagine his surprise when, riding his horse back to the station, he saw the words "Gawne Road" on the newly erected road sign.

*

One cloudy day in the monsoon season, Nityananda was stretched out on the rock. Suddenly, a man approached and demanded to have God revealed to him. The Master told him to go away. When the man became more bombastic, Nityananda grabbed his umbrella and pointed it at the man's toe. Devotees said that the man's dormant kundalini energy, rendered active, must have suddenly risen up his spine to the *brahmarandra* chakra at the top of his head. Anyway, the man screamed and fainted. Reviving, he stumbled to the government hospital for treatment. The doctor in charge reported Nityananda to the police as crazy and possibly dangerous. The police promptly took him before the local magistrate. When Nityananda declared that "This one did nothing," the magistrate asked whether there were witnesses. The Master pointed at the four pillars in the hall and was ordered to jail for insolence.

Soon the prisoner announced his need to urinate. Given a receptacle, he rapidly filled it. Another was supplied, which he again filled to the brim. A water jug was offered next. When it overflowed, the constable hurried off to find the magistrate, who agreed to release this mysterious person.

Meanwhile, the interfering doctor from the hospital went home to discover his wife dancing naked around the house in an apparent state of insanity. The alarmed man rushed first to the police station where, hearing of Nityananda's release, he proceeded to the rock ashram. Begging forgiveness, he was waved away by the Master and returned home to find his wife in her normal state.

In these early days Swami Janananda noted other unusual occurrences around Nityananda. Often, for instance, he would emerge from the water tank following his morning bath with his body and loincloth completely dry. He was also seen walking in the rain without getting wet.

One evening the Master asked for a bottle of arrack, the local fermented beverage. Drinking it, he asked for seven more bottles and finished them in quick succession. Mr. Veera from Kumbla, a heavy drinker himself, could not believe his eyes and asked Nityananda why he did this. He replied that it was for the spirit haunting the rock who, now satisfied, would harm no one in the future.

Visitors to the temple today can still see a small stone in front. During worship, the *arathi* is waved before this stone as well as before Nityananda's statue. It is said that a powerful spirit once inhabited the site. Older Kanhangad residents remember being told as children that those passing the stone without pouring arrack on it would suffer some illness.

※

About a kilometer north of the rock ashram is an area called Kushalnagar. Here in 1931 the Master built a round table out of stone and called it the "Round Table Conference." He would sit at his table and speak of various world issues, relating first the views of other world leaders and then those of Gandhi. Now, at this very time there happened to be an international conference taking place in London. Skeptics among the Master's listeners who checked the newspaper accounts of the "real" Round Table Conference were amazed to find that they coincided exactly with Nityananda's words.

※

As work on the Kanhangad caves neared completion in 1933, Nityananda once again embarked on a period of frequent and often unpredictable travel. Sallying forth from Kanhangad and Ganeshpuri, he might appear in Vajreshwari, Gokarn, Kanheri, Bombay, or anywhere.

One day as he sat under a tree near the rock caves, three local Muslims arrived to stand reverently before him. As he had many Muslim devotees, this was not surprising. Having just returned from their Haj pilgrimage to Mecca, they were asked by the Master what they had seen there. They replied, "We saw you there, Swamiji, and have come to pay homage." Nityananda turned his face with a faint smile on his lips.

Similarly, he was seen in many places around Bombay. Achutamama, a devotee from Udipi, tells how the Master asked him to dig a small grave-like pit in the sands of Chowpati and bury him in it. Alarmed, the man then watched as people unwittingly walked over the spot. After about thirty minutes, Nityananda sprang from the sand and asked his companion to take him home. This happened several times until one day he requested a much deeper pit. When he did not crawl out at the usual time, Achutamama grew anxious but continued to wait. Finally, three hours later Nityananda emerged and casually explained that he had had business in Delhi.

He was a regular visitor to Mrs. Muktabai's Bombay home at this time. Once she and her mother went to the town of Nasik along the Godavari River for a change of climate. While they were away, Nityananda insisted on managing the house for his devotee's husband and attending to the household chores himself.

❧

In 1934 or 1935 he reportedly moved to Akroli near Vajreshwari. Here he repaired the hot spring tanks and the nearby Nath temple. He also built a charity hostel across from the Vajreshwari temple and supervised the construction of a well that is still the site's primary water source. As usual, his followers discovered his whereabouts. One of these faithful was Sitarama Shenoy whom Nityananda asked to open a restaurant across from the Vajreshwari temple.

Others found the Master without even looking. A story goes that Mrs. Muktabai and several Bombay devotees had gathered for a picnic near Vajreshwari. As they ate they spoke of Nityananda, lamenting the fact that three years had passed since they had seen him. At that moment a dark figure emerged from the jungle at the base of Mandakini Mountain and approached the ecstatic group.

In 1957, Mr. Krishnamurthy, a journalist and biographer, wrote the following:

> Two decades ago Nityananda lived for years in a tree in the heart of the Vajreshwari jungle. Once a young man asked him, "Man cannot do the impossible but a yogi can. Won't you awaken the kundalini in me?" Moved by his earnestness, Nityananda touched his spinal cord and, in a split second, the seeker experienced the dynamic charge of the kundalini. The confines of mortal hope blended with the divine light. He felt as if a magnesium wire burned in his head and unfolded a mystery and a wordless music.
>
> When kundalini returns to its spiritual cave, the light is extinguished and the flute broken. Only when one puts the eyes of logic and reason to sleep, can one grasp reality's mysterious flash. For an intellectual understanding of kundalini, we can read books. But in our very own day we have Nityananda as a living emblem of the kundalini process. To him, it is not a mental trap. It is action.
>
> From the moment Nityananda opens the first window of our consciousness, we no longer feel bound by time. Indeed, his greatness lies in time's annihilation. The past becomes a memory. We cease to reach toward future passions. We live in the intuition of the moment. This transforms us from invalid to knower!

SEVEN

Ganeshpuri—The Beginning
1936

Nityananda arrived in Ganeshpuri one morning in 1936. Some people think he came at the goddess Vajreshwari's bidding. We know he did tell Kanhangad devotees of his intention to visit the Bhimeshwar temple, but he said nothing of moving there. In those days Ganeshpuri was surrounded by a dense jungle inhabited by tigers and other wild animals. Access to the temple was via a footpath over a hill known as Mandakini. The area's only other inhabitants lived on the west side of the hill at a sanatorium. There, a doctor had diverted sulfur water from the natural hot springs into specially constructed therapeutic baths for his patients.

When Nityananda reached the Bhimeshwar temple that morning, he was wrapped in a checkered blanket. Thinking him a Muslim, the attending priest's young wife Gangubai refused to let him enter the Hindu shrine. The Master said nothing and retraced his steps to sit by an old well overgrown with vegetation and full of stones.* Late that after-

---

* When the well was later cleared, these stones were touted for their healing power and eagerly collected by ayurvedic physicians.

noon a Vajreshwari devotee arrived and found him still seated by the well. Hearing the tale, the devotee hastened to rectify the mistake. Apologies were immediately offered and soon a temporary structure was built for Nityananda on the temple's west side. It was small, with barely enough room for him to crawl inside and rest.

Before the door stood an ancient pipal tree that was home to many snakes. As he had done with the cobras in Kanhangad, Nityananda issued vibrational orders and they disappeared into the jungle—except for one. The oldest cobra would not leave, preferring death at the Master's hands. The story goes that one day he instructed devotees to stay away and some time later announced that the old snake's wish had been granted. He then ordered villagers to cut down the enormous tree that was now festooned with sacred thread and sprinkled with the red kumkum powder used in Indian rituals.

༺

As word spread of Nityananda's arrival, villagers from surrounding areas began gathering around his hut in the evenings. A large pot of rice porridge, of which the Master would partake, always stood ready for them. Devotees were soon flocking to Ganeshpuri as well. To accommodate them, a building was constructed east of the hot spring water tanks.

At first, due to a lack of potable water, visitors only stayed the day. However, once the old well was refurbished, sulfur water was used for everything. One particularly hot afternoon the Master offered a plate of rice with spicy pickle sauce to a visiting devotee. It so happened that the woman found sulfur water distasteful and declined the food, knowing she would crave something to drink afterward. Nityananda again held out the plate to her, saying, "Don't be concerned. You will drink rain water." Venturing a look at the blue sky, she still ate nothing. Within minutes, however, a solitary cloud appeared overhead and rain poured down. The Master said, "Go and get your water," and she jumped up and collected rainwater for both of them.

～

Within a short period of time, three rooms were added to the temple's south side to form a compound. Today this is called the "old ashram." Nityananda's room with its small cement porch stood in the middle. There were two adjoining rooms that were fully enclosed, one on each side. But the walls of his room only rose seven feet and had a knee-high sliding panel for a door. The dirt yard in front was paved in 1943. Until then he saw devotees in either the building near the bathing tanks or the temple quadrangle.

The only route to the ashram was a winding footpath through the jungle. To reach this path, visitors had to use the neighboring sanatorium's private road. Soon the caretakers there, disgruntled at devotees getting off the bus at the sanatorium gate, began charging them a fee to use the path. This practice continued until, one day, words and blows were exchanged.

Hearing of the incident, Nityananda asked nearby villagers to recruit fifty laborers. The next morning, with the Master working alongside them, they began to clear trees and build a proper road from the ashram to the bus route, which incidentally still conveys regional buses to Ganeshpuri. At the time, however, the district's British magistrate and forest officer received complaints about the unauthorized project. They asked the local forest ranger, who happened to be a devotee, for a complete report. Fearing the worst, and at Nityananda's insistence, the man complied. He described the new road as a public service and stressed the growing influx of devotees needing access to both the ashram and the Bhimeshwar temple. Finally, he concluded that the district benefited considerably from the Master's efforts and really should have undertaken the project itself.

The curious British officials drove to Ganeshpuri after reading the report. Parking well beyond where the Bhadrakali temple now stands, they approached the ashram as Nityananda sat watching them. Suddenly he turned his back to them and they returned to their car. The magistrate later admitted to subordinates that, while rarely moved by charitable thoughts, upon witnessing how this simple yogi worked to help the local poor, he decided to take no further action.

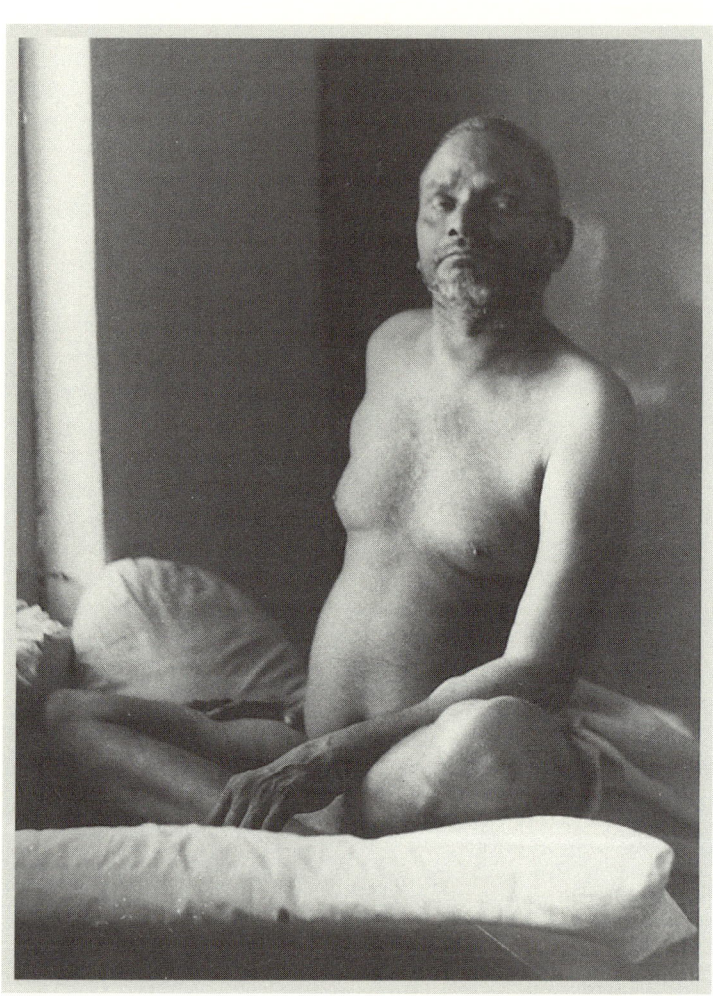

EIGHT

The Old Ashram
1936-1950

One afternoon a visitor took leave of Nityananda, planning to take the footpath through the woods to the Vajreshwari temple. As he walked off, the Master told him not to look back until he reached the temple. Along the way he encountered a cobra in his path but, following the directive, did not turn around. Instead, he waited for the snake to leave. Continuing, he soon heard someone whispering behind him. Once more, controlling his curiosity, he did not look back until he was within sight of the temple. Then, unable to stand the mystery, he turned and saw a gigantic figure with folded arms standing in the river repeating a mantra—which was what he had heard. Quite shaken, he managed to reach the temple where he remained in a dazed state and had to be hospitalized. It took two months for him to fully recover his senses.

There are many such examples of Nityananda's watchfulness. For instance, he always advised devotees not to venture out alone at night. One time, however, Mrs. Muktabai rose after midnight and went to the hot spring tanks to bathe. As she entered, she saw two uncommonly handsome youths run away and disappear inside the temple. She hurriedly returned to the ashram to tell Nityananda, who admonished her for disobeying his instructions. She apologized and then asked about the young men. He replied that they were *sanatkumars*, two of Lord Brahma's four sons born of his mind alone.

In 1965 some of the older devotees told Captain Hatengdi that the young Master often used the phrase "tortoise *drishti*" (or sight) when speaking of his constant mindfulness of their welfare and development. He told them to consider how a mother bird's physical warmth hatches her eggs. In contrast, a mother tortoise climbs onto the beach, lays her eggs, covers them, and returns to the sea, all the while mindful of her eggs. It is her constancy of thought that makes them hatch.

On another occasion, a devotee performing an act of service (*seva*) around the ashram was told to stop at midnight. He did so and then went off to bathe before retiring. En route, he saw an enormous muddy footprint near the statue of Shiva's bull. Though a man of courage, the devotee was shaken by the sight and rushed inside. There the Master waited and immediately asked, "Did you bow before the footprint?" And he quickly returned to do so.

Nityananda said that through time, sages had often frequented the grounds of the old ashram and he considered the hot springs water there to be holy (*koti teertha*). This phrase indicates the waters that saints have bathed in or meditated near. In Ganeshpuri the Master always asked even his oldest devotees to, upon arrival, first bathe in the *kunds*.

∽

Throughout the uncertain light of early morning Nityananda

would maintain a vigil until all the devotees returned from bathing. Once, coming from an early bath, Madhumama, a long-time devotee who sometimes cooked for the Master, encountered him at the ashram entrance. He asked the devotee, "Did you see it?" and pointed to a tiger sitting under a mango tree only twenty yards away. Clearly, the Master was standing guard.

Rajgopal Bhat, a regular visitor for two decades, spoke of a similar incident. In 1949 he brought his family to Bombay for the first time and, on finding no accommodations, was told by Nityananda to stay with a certain Mr. Gandhi in Ganeshpuri. Rising the next morning for a three o'clock visit to the hot springs, he felt himself followed and noticed a faint light behind him. Remembering the Master's perennial advice, he did not look back but continued walking. When he reached the present site of the Bhadrakali temple, the uncertain feeling disappeared. He took his bath and forgot the incident. In the evening Mr. Gandhi visited the ashram. Nityananda told him a tiger had followed Mr. Bhat that morning but his faith in the Master had protected him.

According to another story, Bhagawan Mistry, who handled the ashram's construction work, ran in one evening in obvious agony, shouting that a cobra had bitten him. Nityananda calmly told him to sit down. He asked someone to bring him the snake balm, instructed the bewildered Mistry to rub it on the Master's leg at the spot corresponding to his own wound, and told him to go to sleep. The devotee awoke the next morning fully recovered.

An even more dramatic intervention is related in this story from Dr. Deodhar about Sitarama Shenoy, a Mangalore devotee mentioned earlier in the book. After suffering a severe heart attack, he was taken by his family directly from the hospital to Ganeshpuri. His doctors vehemently protested this action. Arriving in the village, Sitaram was helped from the car and placed on the ground before Nityananda, who proceeded to take his hand and drag him to the river. There Nityananda splashed water on the ailing man's face, telling him that he was fine and could walk back on his own. And so he did, completely recovered. Shortly thereafter, to his doctors' astonishment and at Nityananda's bidding, he opened the restaurant across from the Vajreshwari temple and worked there until his death in 1954. The restaurant is still maintained by his family.

One afternoon Nityananda announced that Narayan Maharaj of Khedgaon was coming. Seeing Achutamama's skepticism, he insisted that the celebrated teacher was in Vajreshwari en route to the ashram. Five minutes later, they heard a car stop to deposit the maharaj, who went directly to the hot springs. Following his ablutions, he approached Nityananda and asked him to cure his skin disorder. But the Master replied, "Inside you are pure. Why bother with the outside?" And the maharaj went away. That evening Nityananda spoke: "Everything was ready for him—the bed made and his head about to touch the pillow. But instead he got up and left." Referring to the spiritual stage previously reached by the maharaj, the Master told devotees that *datta devata siddhi*[1] only lasted fourteen years and required a renewed effort at that point. In contrast, the attainment of divine wisdom carried no such limitation. *Jnana*, he said, was infinite.

A man destined to be a longtime devotee made his first

---

[1]. See the glossary.

visit to Ganeshpuri in 1938. Most people came by bus but, after winning the Goa lottery, Golikeri Lakshman Rao was a rich man. He hired a taxi for the trip and arrived bearing a fruit basket. Nityananda accepted him as well as the fruit. After several visits, he asked Rao to come on a particular date and accompany him on a pilgrimage (*teerthayatra*). As Rao arrived that day, again in a taxi, the villagers fell at Nityananda's feet, pleading with him not to leave. He told them to fall at Rao's feet instead—and they did, much to the devotee's embarrassment. Nityananda motioned for Rao to acknowledge them, and they set off on their journey.

At the train station, over his companion's protests, Nityananda insisted on third-class tickets. And in Poona, their first stop, Nityananda took a hotel room with a bed for Rao—and a space on the floor for himself and a cloth (*chaddar*) for a blanket. The next day they went to Alandi. Here Nityananda encouraged the devotee to follow his usual manner of worship, and so Rao proceeded to the river to bathe before seating himself before the samadhi shrine of Jnaneshwar. Meanwhile, the Master stood for several seconds with his hands at his sides in each corner of the shrine, and then left.

The next stop was to be Pandarpur. But Rao suffered a malaria attack in the night and asked Nityananda's permission to return to Bombay. He made no objection but asked Rao to leave his chaddar for him. Protesting, Rao said he would gladly buy the Master a new one but, again overruled, he sadly departed.

Nityananda traveled on to Pandarpur and other places before returning to Bombay. For several months in early 1939 he lived in the Kanheri caves at Borivli. Adjoining his cave was another where a guru lectured daily on Vedantic philosophy. Focusing on the inconsequential and transitory aspect of the human body, he loudly exhorted his disciples to ignore its many attractions and afflictions. As fate had it, one day the guru was bitten by a snake. The resulting agony was expressed visibly and, as usual, quite vocally on his part. His distressed disciples asked Nityananda to help. While we know his mercy was boundless, the Master nevertheless chuckled and asked if they had already forgotten their guru's words to ignore the body's physical aspects. Then he directed them to splash water from the nearby pond onto the wound. This done, their guru recovered—and immediately came to bow at Nityananda's feet.

Another of the Kanheri caves was occupied by a sanyasi who was a Mahakala worshipper.[2] Following his daily worship he would bring the ritual light and incense (*arathi*) he had waved before his personal shrine and wave it before Nityananda. Taking no notice, the Master told devotees that it was just a sign of the sanyasi's deep devotion.

As always, devotees found Nityananda, and this time they flocked to Kanheri. One was the deeply attached Mrs. Muktabai. She related that one time, in her haste to arrive, she lost her way. Her anxiety grew until an asthmatic old man suddenly appeared and offered to show her the way. As they neared the ashram, he began to lag behind her and at the entrance was nowhere to be seen. Nityananda refused to discuss the incident and reprimanded her soundly for traveling at that hour in such a dangerous region.

Prior to his return to Ganeshpuri, Nityananda told devotees not to come to Kanheri only to see him. He urged them to visit the rock caves built by yogis and sanyasis cen-

---

2. A manifestation of Shiva as time beyond time.

turies earlier and marvel at their arrangements for collecting and storing water.

※

Nityananda returned to Ganeshpuri in 1939, and Rao immediately came to see him. But again, he suffered an attack of malaria. In a fever-induced delirium, he admitted that as a youth he had once received sandwiches from the Muslim sage Baba Jan, which he had thoughtlessly discarded. Hearing the story, the Master shook the ailing man and asked him to repeat it. After listening to it again, he went to the pantry, opened several tins of food, and mixed the contents together on a piece of newspaper. He then carried the huge serving to Rao and ordered him to eat it. The sick devotee did so and immediately fell asleep. He awoke fully recovered, realizing that he had finally atoned for the insult of throwing away a saint's *prasad*.

※

In 1941 Swami Janananda traveled to Ganeshpuri to seek Nityananda's guidance on some financial and construction issues regarding the Kanhangad ashram. On his arrival, and prior to speaking to the Master, he was told to sit down. Within minutes a taxi drove up, a rare occurrence in those days, and Nityananda left, saying he would soon return. And he did—twenty-four hours later in the same taxi. Then, glancing at Swami Janananda, he said, "Go home. Everything is taken care of."

Without a word, Swami Janananda made the return trip, one that involved the usual number of trains and buses. Reaching the ashram, he heard that Nityananda had been there earlier with money and instructions. Let me add that even with today's improved transportation conditions and utilizing the new Netravati Bridge, it is impossible to complete a round trip between Bombay and Kanhangad by taxi in twenty-four hours...

※

Nityananda was never interested in attracting disciples or organizing an ashram. He was egoless in both words and actions. When pressed, he would say, "This one is not flattered when important people come or sad when devotees leave."

Students of other spiritual teachers sometimes came to Ganeshpuri, but the Master always steered them back to their own ashrams. He would tell them that their gurus were quite capable of solving their problems and that it was inappropriate as well as disrespectful to change loyalty on a temporary basis. One morning, as devotees of Shirdi Sai Baba filed before him, Nityananda was heard to shout, "Go back to Shirdi! Does the old man there sit differently than this one does here?"

A similar situation involved the affluent Bhiwandiwalla brothers, then devotees of Narayan Maharaj. When they first learned that Nityananda was in Ganeshpuri, they set off to see him. But when they arrived, Nityananda shouted, "Go back to your guru!" and refused to speak to them. The brothers nevertheless continued to come. It was only when Narayan Maharaj died that the Master finally addressed them and accepted their devotion.

※

There was once a devotee who had lost a flourishing business prior to the Second World War. On his first visit to Ganeshpuri, he kept hearing Nityananda repeat the word "junk" and, try as he might, could not stop thinking about it. When the man returned home, the word still rang in his ears and he went for a walk. Lo and behold, he came upon an auction selling discarded odds and ends to the highest bidder. Without hesitation he bought the entire lot and soon sold it at a profit. Within months he was on his way toward recouping his earlier losses. Within the ashram he was called Raddiwalla, or "the head of junk."

Raddiwalla became a frequent visitor to Ganeshpuri, often bringing his entire family. Always anxious to have Nityananda touch him, he sometimes took the liberty of placing the Master's hand on the head of a relative he wished to have blessed. This annoyed some of the older devotees who had been around since the days in Mangalore. Back then, Nityananda had told them not to prostrate themselves before him, that their inner prayers would reach him. One afternoon Raddiwalla took his leave after placing Nityananda's hand on the head of every member of his family. Unable to contain themselves, the envious devotees asked the Master why he had never favored them in this manner after their many years of devotion. He rebuked them by saying, "A blessing is not given by placing the hand on the head. It is an inner transmission—not an outer demonstration."

One day when the Master complained of fatigue, Mrs. Muktabai admitted her surprise, saying that he rarely left the ashram and spent most of his time resting on the floor of his room or on the bench outside. He quipped, "Yes, but the devotees remember, don't they?" On another occasion he said: "One established in infinite consciousness becomes silent and, while knowing everything, goes about as if knowing nothing. While doing many things in several places, outwardly one appears to do nothing."

❧

One day a new devotee brought his wife to Ganeshpuri. After first greeting Nityananda, they sat down a little apart from the others. Some of the visitors were discussing the building of a small school in the area. Thinking this a good opportunity to contribute something, the husband rose and placed a thousand rupee note on the plate by Nityananda's bench. After resuming his seat, the man was astonished to find his single note transformed into a pile of smaller denomination bills.

❧

Nityananda basked in the spontaneity of life and delighted in saying that things rarely went according to plan—even the best laid ones. After all, he would tell devotees, "God's will always prevails."

In 1949, a devotee from Kerala was filled with dismay when a renowned astrologer announced that the devotee's young wife would soon die due to an affliction of Saturn in her chart. Distraught, the man rushed to Ganeshpuri. As he arrived and sat down, Nityananda turned to him and said, "Saturn is there but so is God." He then told the husband to stay on at the ashram and to perform certain rituals that were never explained. The devotee faithfully followed his instructions to the letter. When the day predicted for the calamity came, it passed without incident—and Nityananda told the happy man to go home.

One morning as Nityananda reclined on his bench with legs outstretched, three stalwart sanyasis appeared in the entrance behind him. One carried a large, brightly-polished trident.[3] Quietly they took a stance behind the Master and waited for him to acknowledge them, but he uttered no sound and made no gesture. Time passed. The visitors grew restless and the watching devotees uncomfortable. Suddenly, the trident bearer thrust it forcefully into midair where it remained of its own accord. Still Nityananda did not turn, but whenever he glanced from the right corner of his eye, the trident swayed slightly. After some moments, Nityananda shook his outstretched foot—and the trident fell with a clatter. Bowing, the sanyasis asked to stay in the ashram for three days. During this time they said they were followers of a powerful guru in the Himalayas. They conceded, however, that Nityananda was himself a great leader of the Nath order of monks (*Matsyendranath*), and demonstrating great respect and affection, they departed with his blessing.

It was around 1942 when Kamath and a friend spent Shivaratri, the annual festival of Shiva, in Ganeshpuri. Staying in rooms opposite the hot spring tanks, they rose at midnight to bathe and then entered the darkness of the Bhimeshwar temple. To their surprise, the beam of their flashlight revealed Nityananda standing with one foot on the linga and repeating, "Shiva is gone, Shiva is gone." And the

---

3. The trident (*trishula*) symbolizes the three powers of the Absolute: will, knowledge, and action. It is often associated with Shiva.

two men knew that for Shiva to have gone he must first have come.

❧

Mrs. Mutkabai once asked Nityananda whether he could see God. His reply was "More clearly than I see you." He also said that physical contact with the teacher was unnecessary. "This one is here, there, and everywhere," he assured. "There is no pinhole where this one will not be found." And a certain incident in the life of G. A. Rao illustrates this.

Rao was the devotee mentioned earlier who had won the lottery. Always generous with his unexpected wealth, he unfortunately lost everything during the war. Nityananda asked a devotee living in the same town as Rao to let the impoverished man stay in his warehouse. One day Rao sadly considered that he did not even have a photo of his guru to wave incense in front of. That night he had a dream. In it, Nityananda had him search the wall above his pillow for a nail hole and instructed him to wave incense before it. The next morning when he awoke, Rao found such a hole and began waving incense before it daily for the duration of his stay.

Some time passed before he finally saw Nityananda in the flesh again. On that occasion the Master remarked that he was enjoying the fragrance of Rao's incense.

❧

One day as visitors from Saurashtra were bowing before Nityananda, one of them began to shiver uncontrollably. Afterward a devotee took him aside to ask why he had reacted so. The man said that before leaving his village he had seen the Master in a nearby cave and was shocked to find him here as well. That evening when the devotee remarked on the unlikelihood of such an occurrence, Nityananda replied, "Anything is possible."

Anything is possible. To Nityananda this was abundantly clear. When, in the mid-1950s, he asked Madhumama to go to Badrinath, the devotee stopped over in Rishikesh. There he was approached by a tall stranger who, in passing, warned him in Kanarese: "Don't eat anything offered by a sanyasi on your way to Badrinath. Only eat temple food." Madhumama was mystified by both the message and the messenger. How would anyone know that he understood Kanarese and was en route to Badrinath? Turning to ask him, he found only empty space.

On his subsequent return to Ganeshpuri, he told fellow devotees that when he bowed at Kedarnath he felt as if his head touched the body of the Master. Some devotees laughed, but Nityananda remarked, "There is no need to doubt his experience. The body without the head (Munda) is in Kedarnath while the head without the body (Runda) is in Pashupathinath. If Shiva's body can lie in Kedarnath and his head in Pashupathinath, then a devotee should not be surprised to feel Nityananda's body anywhere."

❦

M. Hegde, a young relative of Sitarama Shenoy, was posted to Bombay during the Second World War as an apprentice in the Naval Dockyard. On his regular visits to Ganeshpuri, he was sometimes asked to prepare the Master's tea. During one visit to the jungle ashram, he found himself questioned by Nityananda. Did he wish to improve his prospects? Did he know about the government-sponsored Bevin Boy's Training Program in Great Britain? Hegde said he had read about it in the newspaper but thought himself ineligible because quotas were determined by province and he was not really from Bombay.

The Master told him to think big and apply anyway. The boy did and was accepted. However, at his medical examination, the local doctor contested his candidacy and declared him medically unfit. When Hegde hurried to Ganeshpuri, Nityananda again advised him to think bigger and appeal the decision. Hegde therefore wrote to the surgeon general and received an appointment. Puzzled at the sight of a healthy young man standing before him, the surgeon general asked the local doctor to explain his ruling. Because he was unable to do so satisfactorily, the decision was overturned.

During his year of training in Great Britain, Hegde began dating an English woman. One time, while the two were strolling in a park, Hegde suddenly saw an apparition of the Master before him. His stern face seemed to say, "Was this why you came to this place?" The apparition disappeared and Hegde began sweating profusely even though it was winter. The look on his face apparently was startling enough to make the woman end their relationship on the spot.

When he returned to India, Hegde went directly to Ganeshpuri to ask Nityananda what he should do next. The Master told him to put on a suit and walk up and down one of Bombay's major commercial streets from ten in the morning to five in the afternoon. This was a tall order, but the young devotee resolved to follow his instructions to the letter. Exhausted, he later returned home and wondered how he would get a job by pacing up and down. Nevertheless, the next day he faithfully repeated his vigil. By noon he found himself staring aimlessly at a notice board outside the Macropolo shop. From the corner of his eye, he saw a foreigner enter the shop. Exiting some time later, the foreigner was surprised to see Hegde still staring at the notices. He asked the young man what he was doing and Hegde admitted that he was looking for work. The stranger inquired into his qualifications and whether he was prepared to go to Calcutta that night. Gulping, Hegde said yes and followed the man to the Lakshmi office building where he accepted a good opening position plus traveling expenses.

Predictably, Hegde caught the first train to Ganeshpuri. A hundred yards from the ashram, he could hear Nityananda shouting at him to return to the station immediately if he intended to catch the train for Calcutta. And joyously saluting the Master from that distance, Hegde set out for his new job.

Nityananda's understanding of life was light years beyond the people around him. Time after time, someone would express concern or sorrow about an event only to have the Master explain, sometimes in exasperation, that many things occur beneath life's apparent surface. Stories abound, of course.

Captain Hatengdi's mother was among those who first sought out Nityananda. In 1924, however, she turned instead to Swami Siddharud in Hubli, being quite taken with the many miracles attributed to him. Two decades later, as her son's connection with Nityananda evolved, he wrote to his mother and invited her to the ashram. And so it passed that in February 1944, accompanied by a brother and his family, she traveled to Ganeshpuri. Upon seeing her, and with characteristic brevity, Nityananda asked,

"How long?"

Unprepared for this greeting, the woman mumbled, "Perhaps twenty years."

"No," came his reply. "Twenty-two. Anyway, where is Siddharud now?"

"He is no more."

"Where has he gone? Can you see him when you close your eyes?" he asked. When she said yes, he repeated, "Are you so certain he has gone anywhere?"

The Hatengdi family was assigned a room near the baths for the night. That evening Nityananda visited, sitting without saying a word. When one woman quietly asked about his silence, another said that he must be meditating because it was sunset. The Master immediately spoke, "All that was over in the mother's womb."

Another time a couple arrived in Ganeshpuri. After first bathing, they were arranging to prepare a meal for the Master when they saw him rush across the compound. He shouted at them to leave at once. The startled devotees hurriedly packed and left—just catching a bus to make the rail connection at Bassein. The instant they arrived home, a fierce gale began to rattle the shutters and windows. It was a precursor to a formidable storm that severed railway connections in the region. In fact, had the couple not caught that particular bus and train, they would have been stranded in Ganeshpuri for ten days.

Once again a hardship proved to be a blessing when a devotee and his wife arrived in Ganeshpuri for a few days.

After settling in, they hired a horse-drawn carriage to take them to Vajreshwari. But as the wife climbed into the vehicle, she fell and broke her ankle. Witnessing the occurrence, Nityananda told the husband to take her to a certain bone-setter in Bombay as opposed to the hospital. When an anxious friend of the couple asked Nityananda how such a thing could happen in Ganeshpuri, he replied, "She has young children. A fatal accident would have brought distress to them." It was clear to everyone that a fatal accident had been averted.

Around 1950, Dr. Deodhar recalls seeing two cars arrive. From one car servants emerged carrying bedding and headed for the ashram's back door. It seemed that the Bhiwandiwalla family was preparing to stay for some time. Family members emerged from the other car and walked toward the main entrance. One man gingerly carried an inert child in his outstretched arms. Not ten minutes later, the servants returned to the cars with the bedding. Next came the family, the same man still holding the child. The entourage drove off and Dr. Deodhar hurried inside. There he learned that the child suffered from pneumonia and had been unconscious for three days. The family brought the child before Nityananda and begged him to open the child's eyes. Passing his hand over the small face, the child's eyes opened, but moving his hand back, the child's eyes closed. Nityananda then told the family to perform the last rites because the child was dead.

Mistry had been in charge of the ashram's construction work for many years and felt comfortable around his guru. Without thinking, he remarked how unfortunate it was that the child had died in Nityananda's presence. Angrily the Master said, "What do you know about it? This is the fourth time that the child has come from its mother's womb seeking liberation. It has wanted freedom but karmic law has dragged it down again and again into the same family. Now fulfilled, this soul will not have to return." Overcome by curiosity, Dr. Deodhar later questioned a family member, who confirmed that four infants had died shortly after birth—the last one only after receiving darshan from Nityananda.

In another instance, a Bombay couple had their first child late in life. When he contracted smallpox, the parents rushed him to Ganeshpuri. There they placed their beloved son at Nityananda's feet in full view of a group of devotees and ashram children. Aware of the risk to those present, the Master ordered the couple to take their sick child home immediately. Then Nityananda stood up and entered his own room. For ten days he stayed inside seeing no one, until one morning he emerged and walked directly to the hot springs to bathe. Following him, anxious devotees noticed a number of skin eruptions on his body. Later they learned that in Bombay the sick child had miraculously recovered.

※

The following story occurred some time before Dr. Deodhar became a devotee. On his jungle estate near Panvel stood a small shrine to Shiva. Installed by his family at this shrine was a certain Swami Ramananda who performed the daily rituals. Once a week the monk went to the Deodhar compound to collect supplies, and one time he arrived as the family was deciding whether to escavate an old rubble-filled basement that lay directly beneath the present house. Listening to the discussion, Swami Ramananda excitedly said the basement held a golden treasure guarded by a large cobra, and he offered to retrieve it for them. Rather doubtful, Dr. Deodhar said they were not seeking treasure—only a basement. But the family agreed to let the swami supervise the project.

Two days of digging passed without producing any sign of a basement. Meanwhile the family grew increasingly anxious, fearing that the house might collapse. Swami Ramananda pleaded for one more day, and spent the night in the trench breathing so loudly that no one slept. The next morning he climbed out and said they could replace the escavated dirt because nothing would ever materialize. Angrily, he added that a certain *langotiwalla* (literally "one in charge of the loincloths") was preventing their success, and he would go to Ganeshpuri and demand satisfaction.

The swami said he had known this langotiwalla in Rishikesh. He recalled that in those days Nityananda was already a powerful yogi known to lie on the bank of the Ganges for long periods of time without taking food or water. He explained that, in the case of the basement, Nityananda had obviously "blinded" Swami Ramananda's powers (*siddhis*). In short, it was not that the basement with its treasure did not exist; it was simply that Nityananda was not allowing the swami to find it.

Now it seemed that Dr. Deodhar was already in the habit of visiting holy men residing in Maharashtra. He had even heard about Nityananda from his patients and wanted to accompany Swami Ramananda to Ganeshpuri. However, when they missed their travel connections in Thana, he returned home. Swami Ramananda continued on, promising to tell the doctor later about his intended confrontation.

Swami Ramananda returned a few days later, a changed man. He admitted to having been severely chastised by

Nityananda. "This is the third time you have used your siddhis in recent years," he told him. "You have far to go in your spiritual work and should know that you will never succeed by using your powers for vain and selfish reasons. Why did you do it?" Swami Ramananda meekly replied that he was only trying to express his gratitude to the Deodhar family. But Nityananda admonished him again, saying that it was the wrong way to do it. He then ordered him to move to a certain spot on the Narmada River and continue his personal practice. The humbled swami left immediately after telling his story and the family never saw him again. Dr. Deodhar felt compelled to meet Nityananda and became a lifelong devotee.

※

There is still an air of mystery around Nityananda's age, background, and movements. For instance, the only information known about his visits to the northern regions is that he traveled north between the ages of 12 and 16 or so, after leaving his foster father in Benares. In 1944 he told devotees of his presence when the ancient Ananteshwar temple was built. He described himself then as having an unkempt beard and matted hair. The confines of time and space did not appear to affect him.

NINE

The Old Ashram
1950-1956

Devotees gathered late one evening in 1950 on the west side of the ashram. Here Nityananda sat on a small ledge bordering a six-foot drop into the darkening fields behind him. Silence prevailed. Suddenly in the distance a pair of bright eyes appeared and, weaving its way slowly through the fields, a tiger came up to the ledge and stopped. The animal then rose lightly on its haunches and rested its forepaws on Nityananda's shoulders. Calmly the Master reached up with his right hand and stroked the tiger's head. Satisfied, the tiger jumped back down and disappeared into the night. Later Nityananda observed that as the vehicles of the Goddess Vajreshwari tigers should be expected around her temple. He also said that wild beasts behave like lambs in the presence of enlightened beings.

Many stories tell of his uncanny ability to understand animals. In Udipi he once told its captors to release a certain caged bird because it constantly cursed them. Another time he reassured a frightened devotee that a nearby cobra was too busy chanting to harm anybody. Others remember a devotee who always came for darshan accompanied by his pet parrot. And in May 1944 Captain Hatengdi heard Nityananda say that a bird told him it would rain in three days, and rain it did.

⁂

Among the many distinguished visitors seen in Ganeshpuri was a certain swami from Shirali. This enlightened yogi was the ninth guru of a small community that had demonstrated an enviable performance record in all spheres of endeavor for nearly a century. A shining example of kindness and humility but too mild mannered to exercise his authority, the gentle guru found himself dominated by a committee of lay advisors. For many years he had expressed a desire to visit Ganeshpuri but the trip was always thwarted by the committee.

Finally asserting himself in 1951, the swami departed on his pilgrimage. He was accompanied by a Shirali entourage that included three Nityananda devotees—Mrs. Muktabai, her brother, and his wife. The trip's organizers, still unenthusiastic about the trip, drove the swami to nearby Akroli where they started to hurry him from the car to the nearby hot springs. But their guru asked where Nityananda was. Hesitating, they admitted to being several miles from Ganeshpuri. The swami demanded to continue on, saying he would only bathe at the ashram. And so the group continued on.

Now it seemed that on the previous day Nityananda announced that a visitor would arrive at eleven the next morning. He then asked a devotee to heat some cow's milk and set it aside. When the swami and his entourage arrived, precisely at eleven, they proceeded directly to the hot springs. However, Mrs. Muktabai ran to the Master's room and excitedly exclaimed, "Deva, our Swamiji has come!" Nityananda replied, "Everything is known. Milk has been put aside. Place a chair on the temple's outer veranda, put a shawl on it, and offer the milk to the swami."

And so it passed that the swami had his bath, he worshipped at the Bhimeshwar temple, and he gratefully accepted the milk. He then rose and proceeded to the ashram's western hall. As the swami and his lay followers passed the room where Nityananda sat, the lay followers, still determined to prevent a face-to-face meeting, silently bowed before the Master's door and conveniently blocked him from view. Oddly, the swami no longer asked about Nityananda. He simply sat in the hall repeating over and over, "We are feeling blissful here and do not feel like leaving." (To avoid saying "I," *mathadipathis* customarily refer to themselves in the first person plural.) Although pleased that he seemed to have forgotten about Nityananda, the lay advisors still worried. They tried to hurry him by saying that he would miss evening services in Shirali if he did not leave immediately. The swami replied, "Why the concern about being late for one service? We are in a state of bliss and do not feel like leaving." However, eventually they persuaded him to leave, and the motorcade departed.

Staying behind, Mrs. Muktabai again rushed to Nityananda's room, this time to say with sorrow that the swami had left without seeing him. The Master replied, "You are wrong—the meeting did occur. But his coming to Ganeshpuri was unnecessary. It could have happened anywhere and so many people tried to prevent it." She then knew that the encounter had been on a subtle level, leaving the swami in a state of bliss and immobility. She also realized that the Master himself had made the swami temporarily forget about him. Several other Ganeshpuri devotees belonged to this community and Nityananda had always told them that the swami was a good sanyasi and a true yogi.

When the party from Shirali was ten miles from Ganeshpuri, the swami awoke as if from a reverie and exclaimed: "Oh, but we did not meet Nityananda!" His advisors responded that they had driven too far to turn back. To this the swami said, "I believe he came to Shirali once but we were quite young at the time. We have long desired to meet him." But as was their custom, his advisors chose to ignore the swami's gentle hint.

Meanwhile Mrs. Muktabai's brother was upset with the subterfuge. He returned to Ganeshpuri the next day and told Nityananda what had occurred on the return drive, adding that he personally would bring the swami to meet him. But the Master replied, "It is unnecessary because the meeting took place. Moreover the good man suffers from diabetes and is unfit for another tiring journey. Remember that he is a Mathadipathi and must listen to his people."

༄

One day Mr. Mudbhatkal's Muslim landlord told him that he had always wanted to meet Nityananda but ill health prevented him from traveling. The devotee promised on his forthcoming visit to Ganeshpuri to bring his landlord some prasad. However, when he found a large group of visitors from Bombay seated before the Master, he timidly decided to wait until another day to mention his landlord. At the end of his visit the devotee went to bow before the Master, still conscious of his broken promise. As he turned to go, Nityananda called him back and purposefully handed him a coconut. His landlord's desire was fulfilled.

Similarly, a devotee from Santa Cruz tells of a childhood journey to Ganeshpuri in the company of a group that included a follower of U. Maharaj. Learning of the disciple's intended visit, his guru gave him a coconut to offer Nityananda. When the group neared the ashram, it found Nityananda leaning against the wooden gate waiting. The moment he saw them he said, "The coconut has been received"—as if to say a thought was as good as a deed. And we know that in the Mangalore days he told devotees that inner salutations expressed with purity of feeling and motive (*shuddha bhavana*) made physical obeisance unnecessary.

꙳

During this time Shankar Tirth, a sanyasi who had wandered for years without finding inner peace, first appeared. Hearing one day about Nityananda, he journeyed to Ganeshpuri where, upon receiving darshan, he finally found happiness. Asking the Master where he should stay, he was told to occupy the nearby Nath temple that Nityananda had restored two decades earlier. Shankar Tirth did so but the next morning, visibly shaken, said he had experienced such frightening nightmares of attacking cobras telling him to leave—that he asked to live elsewhere. Instead Nityananda told him to go back to the temple and announce on whose orders he was there. The sanyasi did this but returned the following day with the same story. Again Nityananda told him to go back and tell the threatening forces who had sent him. This time his announcement produced peace and quiet.

A year or two later the shankaracharya who had initiated Shankar Tirth into his particular order of monks was camped at Banaganga. When he sent word for the sanyasi to report for final initiation, Shankar Tirth asked Nityananda if he should go. He was told that it was unnecessary, and so he informed the shankaracharya that he would not come.

∽

Another shankaracharya visited Ganeshpuri in the mid-fifties. Details of his visit reached Captain Hatengdi in an unusual way. In fact, it was in 1977 at a *harikatha*, which is a scriptural story told in song and narrative, that he heard the story:

The Shankaracharya of Puri was spending his *chaturma* in Bombay. Traditionally, a chaturma was the four months of monsoon during which a wandering sadhu would stay in one place, but these days it referred to a period of special study. At the end of his time there he visited the Dattatreya shrine in Vakola, where he expressed a desire to visit the Vajreshwari temple. Having just written a book on Shakti, he wanted to visit the shrine of the goddess before it was published. The then young harikatha performer was hired to drive two men, the elderly shankaracharya and a shastri learned in the scriptures, to Vajreshwari. The old swami was not very strong and had to be helped up the steps leading to the shrine. Afterward, the shankaracharya suddenly uttered a desire to see Nityananda and the three companions found themselves unexpectedly en route to Ganeshpuri.

When they arrived, the Master was resting on his narrow bench with a few people seated before him. The three new visitors quietly joined the others. Silence reigned. After some time the scholar stood up and announced who they were. He said that the shankaracharya had written a book on Shakti and that they had come for Nityananda's blessing. No one else spoke, and the silence continued. At some point the Master raised his head and nodded to an attending devotee, who left and quickly reappeared with a mysteriously prepared tray of fresh flowers, fruit, and coconuts. The attendant respectfully placed the tray before the shankaracharya and withdrew. Although it was clear that Nityananda had been expecting the holy man, he still did not speak. Several minutes passed before the scholar again stood up, this time to say that what was transpiring in silence was new to him. He nevertheless recognized that the flowers and fruit represented Nityananda's blessing and announced that his party would take its leave. Bowing deeply, the three visitors left the silent ashram.

༄

In 1954, G.L. Rao was staying with Shankar Tirth in the Nath temple opposite the Vajreshwari temple. One afternoon Godarvarimata, a holy woman from Sakori, drove up to the temple and asked whether she could be taken to Ganeshpuri. Shankar Tirth asked Rao to accompany her. They found Nityananda resting in his room with his feet extended onto the cement platform. Rao announced the arrival of the visitor, who sat down near his feet, and Nityananda grunted in acknowledgment. Wishing to be hospitable, Rao asked whether he could bring Godivarimata something to drink, and Nityananda said yes. While Rao was away, the Master came out of his room and sat on the platform. Godarvarimata stayed for two days, later saying that Nityananda had given her the darshan of her own guru. She had originally come to ask Nityananda to grace a Vedic ceremony in Bombay with his physical presence. He refused, saying he would observe the ritual from Ganeshpuri—but she continued to press her invitation. When finally he replied that "one has to come only if one is not there already," she stopped asking. Later it was reported that on the final day of the yajna the holy woman was granted the darshan of Nityananda.

※

In 1954, Sitarama Shenoy suffered a heart attack in Vajreshwari and died. Grief stricken and inconsolable, his wife was determined to take the body to Ganeshpuri. Accordingly she hired a car, had the body placed in it, and proceeded toward the ashram. A quarter mile away, the car stalled and would not start up again. At this point the driver announced that he would neither repair the car in the dark nor help carry the body the remaining distance. Undeterred, the widow left the body with the driver and set off for the ashram on foot. When she was still some two hundred yards from the gate, she heard Nityananda shouting, "Go back and perform the last rites!" She pleaded with him but was ordered away.

The devotee Rao was present that evening and asked Nityananda why he had not revived her husband as he had done some years earlier. The Master responded that their children had been young then and needed a father, and in compassion the Divine Force worked that way. However, present conditions were different. His interference, he said, would cause people to stop going to Chandanwadi, Bombay's crematorium, and come to Ganeshpuri instead.

※

Nityananda often tested a devotee's mettle, as in the instance of a Brahman devotee who came weekly to read the scriptures aloud in the Master's presence. After several visits he asked to be cured of his tubercular condition and constant cough. Nityananda agreed and told him to eat a small frog fried in ghee every day. A strict vegetarian, the Brahman was horrified—but having asked for Nityananda's help, he dutifully complied with the instructions. Soon his lungs improved and he developed a taste for frogs in the bargain.

The Master never took credit for the endless instances of healing that occurred around him. In fact, he often directed devotees to rely on their own traditional medical physicians. When pressed, he attributed everything to the Divine Force. He would say: "This one has no desire to do good deeds. Everything that happens does so through the will of God."

※

Nityananda was tolerant of his devotees' humanness; his actions indicated that one's heart was free to turn to God only after the basic human needs were fulfilled. He made no demands, issued no commandments, and frequently concerned himself with their worldly comfort. In return, all he asked was that followers be prepared to receive that which he offered in such abundance.

This is a story of an attorney from the distant state of Kerala who regularly visited Ganeshpuri on weekends. As the years passed, however, the devotee felt keenly the loneliness of his unmarried state and finally announced he wanted a wife. Listening, Nityananda pointed to the surrounding throng and said, "Take one from here." The prospective bridegroom instantly froze, concerned that his mention of a private problem had triggered a casual response. Bewildered, he sat as the people around him slowly dispersed until only one man remained, likewise from Kerala. Eyeing the attorney, he told Nityananda that he and his wife were having difficulty arranging a suitable match for their daughter. Nityananda pointed to his devotee.

Everything seemed settled until their families sent the potential couple's horoscopes to a group of astrologers who unanimously pronounced the match unsuitable. When informed of this, Nityananda without a glance at the offending charts pointed out that a certain aspect nullified the negative signs correctly discerned by the astrologers. When this information was relayed to Kerala, the astrologers agreed, amazed at their failure to notice this vital detail, and the couple married.

༄

A longstanding devotee from the Mangalore days was a woman whose ill-tempered husband never allowed her to handle any family financial matters. In fact, she had never dared to ask him for money. Then one day following their recent move to Bombay, the wife asked her husband for some rupees. He demanded to know why. She replied that she wanted to visit nearby Ganeshpuri and he quipped, "And what will you achieve by going there?" Seconds later he literally threw a five-rupee note at her. Normally she would never have touched money so humiliatingly offered, but determined to see Nityananda she picked up the note and departed at once.

Reaching the old ashram at a little past noon, she found the devotees restless and the atmosphere tense. The Master had not taken his afternoon meal and as a result no one had eaten. They told her that when he was approached earlier about his food, Nityananda had become very upset and sent the questioner away. The devotees implored the woman to speak to him, and she approached the small room where he sat across from the Krishna temple. Seeing her, the Master visibly relaxed and asked, "Well he hasn't changed yet." His faithful devotee replied, "I don't know whether people ever change their inborn habits—but I have brought some food for you. Will you eat now?" And he did.

୨୦

Late one evening in 1955, Nityananda asked his attendants to count the money in the Krishna temple donation box. When told the amount, he asked them to remove all but a quarter of it. The next morning worshippers found the box broken and the money stolen. When informed, the Master nodded. He said that on the previous night he had noticed a starving man silently praying for enough money in the temple box to feed him. And so Nityananda obliged him with an adequate amount.

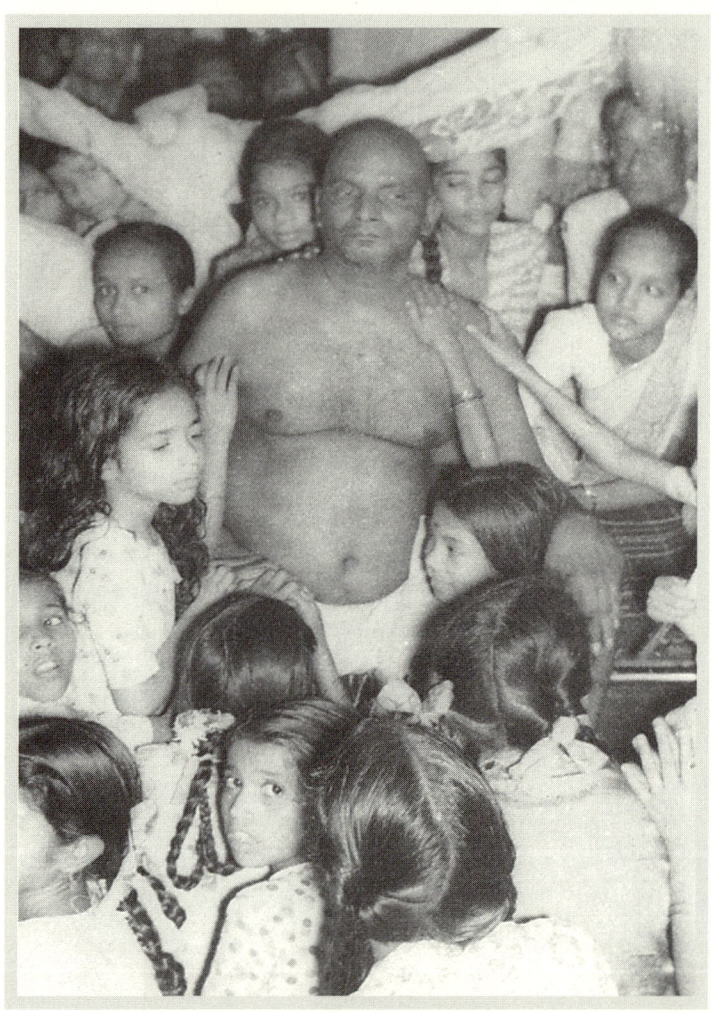

TEN

The New Ashram at Kailas
1956-1961

In 1956 a new ashram at Ganeshpuri was inaugurated and named "Kailas" after the Himalayan mountain home of Shiva. Here Nityananda lived for five more years—until two weeks before his mahasamadhi. Changes accompanied the new living situation. The Master's devotee attendants now monitored access to his private quarters and put darshan on a schedule. Visitors wishing to see Nityananda at other times were forced to make special arrangements.

Early one evening Nityananda sat in the middle of the inner platform with a pile of pillows at his left. Before him a window revealed steps leading to the terrace. Suddenly the young head of an important monastery in Udipi appeared at the entrance. He was accompanied by a number of followers, one of whom announced to Nityananda's seated devotees that their swami required a mat to sit on. The devotees watched the Master for a clue as to how to proceed—but he continued to gaze out the window without acknowledging the visitor in any way. Finally the swami respectfully pushed the pillows against the wall and seated himself on the platform's edge. He then addressed Nityananda in Kanarese.

"Why do they call you God?" he asked.

Looking to his left, the Master replied, "Everyone is a God including yourself and those sitting here."

"But they call you an incarnation," insisted the young man.

Nityananda answered, "Does an incarnate ever make such a pronouncement? Does a *jnani* ever project himself as enlightened?"

"Yes, Krishna does in the Bhagavad Gita."

"No, Vyasa does so in telling the story—Krishna does not."

"But," the swami argued, "Krishna showed the universal form of God to Arjuna. It is recorded in the Gita!"

"How can the Absolute's form be seen or shown?" the Master said. "Vyasa wrote it to inculcate faith among the devout."

Trying to open an intellectual debate, the youth then raised certain points mentioned in the Gita. However, always impatient of such dry discussions, Nityananda waved him aside, saying: "What is in the Gita? From beginning to end, it is simply advice to renounce, renounce, renounce! To renounce worldliness and its inherent desires."

Considerably moved, the swami rose and thanked Nityananda for his darshan. But when he left, two of his followers stayed behind. The Master shrugged and said, "When there is yoga, there will be darshan."

A week later, the Master mentioned his young visitor. He hinted that in a previous incarnation the swami had been the elderly priest from Udipi who, recognizing the then youthful Nityananda's divine presence, had ordered the villagers not to harass him. This past connection had brought him to Ganeshpuri and Nityananda foresaw a bright future for him.

*

On another occasion, a small band of renunciates came and stood before him as he rested on the inner platform of his room. Nityananda nodded to them from his sleeping posture and they left without a word. When some of the devotees present expressed their surprise at not recognizing the renunciates, the Master said devotees did not just reside in Ganeshpuri. He said some lived in jungles, some in cities, and others in foreign lands.

*

Mrs. Kaikini of Dadar was a faithful follower of a great scholar who held audiences spellbound during his brilliant lectures on Jnaneshwar's famous translation of the Bhagavad Gita. Each year she was among those who accompanied him to Pandarpur on an annual pilgrimage known as Wari. Because Mrs. Muktabai occasionally attended these lectures, she became friends with Mrs. Kaikini and eventually invited her to Ganehspuri. However, Mrs. Kaikini demurred, saying that it did not sound like an atmosphere she would enjoy. She admitted hearing that Nityananda was taciturn, gave no meaningful talks, and often rebuked visitors.

Some time later, just before the annual Wari, Mrs. Kaikini missed one of her scholar's regular lectures. Instead she went to a talk by a rival who, new on the scene, was beginning to attract a following. As fate would have it, her scholar/teacher had both noticed Mrs. Kaikini's absence and heard of her attendance at the other lecture. He angrily proclaimed that she was never again welcome in his presence or at the Wari.

When Mrs. Kaikini heard this, she was deeply shocked. To be punished so severely for what she considered a minor transgression was more than she could bear. Friends feared for her mental balance and Mrs. Muktabai again asked her to come to Ganeshpuri. This time Mrs. Kaikini agreed.

Their party arrived to find Nityananda sitting on his bench. When Mrs. Muktabai told him what had happened, he responded with characteristic brevity. "In divine wisdom (*jnana*) how can there be difference (*bheda*)?" The two women took this to mean that if Mrs. Kaikini was truly listening to the saint Jnaneshwar, would it matter which lecture she was at? Then the Master pointed to the ground and shouted, "Besides, this is Pandarpur. There is no need to go in Wari!" He repeated this and as he did, Mrs. Kaikini's relief was immediate and she returned home calmed and at peace.

The following year as the month for the Wari approached, her anxiety returned, and she decided to go to Pandarpur on her own. But when she started to pack she fell ill. By the time she was well enough to travel, it was too late. The following year followed a similar pattern. Again, as she began to pack she became ill. Only then did she recognize the significance of Nityananda's words—and from that moment she no longer felt compelled to attend the Wari. Some years later she suddenly weakened and took to her bed. Stopping her son from rushing for a doctor, she said "Please don't. I see Nityananda standing there and he has come to take me." Within minutes she passed away.

Narayan Shetty, popularly called Sandow Shetty, was a familiar figure in Ganeshpuri in the last ten years of Nityananda's life. He was a big, gregarious man looked up to in the ashram—although he sometimes went too far acting the buffoon. Now it happened that he was quite fond of fruit, especially those brought as offerings. Often he would seek the Master's permission with silent gestures and then slyly slip the best ones aside for himself. When a few devotees objected to such audacity, Nityananda retorted, "Never mind. His desires are simple—let him have the fruit."

Some years after the Master's passing, Sandow was hospitalized following surgery. Captain Hatengdi, going to visit his friend, found him semi-conscious and speaking as if to Nityananda. "Remember, Master, that you promised me a place," he muttered. "Don't forget." And to the shock of the doctors who expected a full recovery, he died.

Once a famous singer visited Ganeshpuri at the invitation of a devotee. While fans and critics alike considered the man outstanding in his field, they agreed that he was also a little arrogant. Upon entering the ashram to perform, the man found a group of tribal people seated around the Master reclining on his bench as usual. Mud floor, an uncultured audience, and Nityananda's apparent indifference instantly upset the artist who decided his talents were wasted on this gathering. Without a word, he turned and went to his room. Later that evening a woman from a distinguished school of music arrived and performed for over an hour. Overhearing her, the disgruntled artist decided that he would perform the next day. To his dismay, however, that morning he could not utter a single note. He fearfully approached Nityananda who said, "Sing? Why not? God gave you the voice—sing his praises. Why should you care who hears and who does not?" Instantly the man's voice returned—and he burst into song.

Please note that Indian music is an ancient science intended to enhance the individual's communion with the Infinite. Fame and wealth are incidental to its spiritual aspect. For this reason most songs relate in some way to reuniting the individual with the Supreme.

※

A year or two after K.S. Lulla began visiting Ganeshpuri, Nityananda took him aside. He told the attorney to go to Kanhangad and then to Dharmasthala to receive darshan at the famous Manjunatha Temple. He also told him to travel by air. This was the devotee's first trip to that part of the country and he planned it with care. He first proceeded to Kanhangad and from there to Mangalore. He then intended to take an early taxi to Dharmasthal and return to Mangalore in time for his 11:30 a.m. flight to Bombay. Accordingly, he rose, procured a taxi, and arrived at Dharmasthal at six in the morning. But when he tried to enter the Jain shrine for darshan, he was stopped. The attendant priest informed him that he could receive darshan only after first participating in the ritual *puja*—which would occur at noon. Lulla explained his predicament but the priest was adamant, explaining that tradition required this protocol of even the highest in the land. However Lulla persisted and was finally taken before the hereditary head of the temple, who simply repeated the temple rules. Nityananda's devotee in turn repeated his plea, saying, "Bhagawan sent me for

Lord Manjunatha's darshan but my return flight is at 11:30. If you cannot help me I will go back and explain to Bhagawan why I did not receive darshan." Intrigued, the gentleman asked to whom he referred. When Lulla said "Nityananda of Ganeshpuri," the priest was told to let him enter the temple at once.

Lulla quickly returned to Ganeshpuri to tell his tale. To his surprise, however, the devotees already knew of the successful pilgrimage. He then learned that at the exact moment of his entry into the Jain temple in Dharmasthal the Master had smiled in Ganeshpuri, announcing, "Lulla is having darshan of Manjunatha."

～

This incident is unusual because Nityananda seldom urged participation in traditional ritual or public worship. Instead he often said that for it to lead to liberation devotion should not be demonstrative but practiced secretly. "Gupta bhakti—mukti!"

Once a devotee spoke of her spiritual experiences to friends in Bombay and implied that she was developing rapidly. On her next visit to Ganeshpuri the Master asked, "What do you do when you season food? Don't you cover it for a time and let it simmer?" This, he explained, allows the flavor to permeate the dish rather than escape into the air. Similarly, spiritual experiences should be kept private until one has evolved enough to speak of them without arousing the ego.

A cooking analogy is not surprising considering Nityananda's knowledge of the subject. He sometimes instructed a cook on how to grind the masala and what spices to use. It was customary for his devotees in Ganeshpuri to each prepare a dish as a daily offering to him. And Nityananda would always know if an ingredient was missing or make suggestions about blending spices or some aspect of its preparation. He once told a devotee that as a person became more spiritually evolved, he or she would instinctively be able to cook well and combine ingredients in the right proportions without having to measure them.

Nityananda's personal knowledge of the culinary art was legendary. G.L. Rao recalls that the Master once prepared a superb festival dinner for him. Serving Rao most of the food, he saved a little for himself on a sheet of newspaper. This he mixed with some curry, ate a few bites while still standing, and then threw away the paper. Captain Hatengdi had a similar experience in 1945 when Nityananda prepared some rice and a regional potato dish peculiar to his devotee's native region. Carrying it to the guest room, he handed it to him. Moving a discreet distance away, the self-conscious devotee began to eat as the Master watched. Though delicious, it was an enormous portion and only after some time did Nityananda suggest that he could stop eating. Another year passed until one day, as they sat together, the Master remarked, "It is good to know how to cook." Captain Hatengdi took it as a casual utterance until thirty years later he found himself forced to learn the elements of cooking.

❧

Nityananda could be very modern in his views. Once a devotee with a growing family brought his fifth and youngest child to Ganeshpuri. Oddly enough, no one else was around. The Master gave the baby his blessing and played with him for a while—and then turned to address the father. "Why must you reproduce like the cat family? Go and have an operation."

Another time, on an evening in 1947, he broke ashram silence to speak about Prohibition. "How is it possible to stop a poor man from drinking?" he demanded. "What can one offer a weary man who trudges home every night with little to feed his family and even greater debts? How should he forget his worries and fall asleep? Currently, every household in this region brews its own liquor from plantains. Make drunkenness a crime—but not drinking. Until people are properly fed and have healthy recreation, drinking will exist."

In another instance a mutton shopkeeper decided his hereditary avocation was unclean. After much thought, he shut down his butcher shop and reopened it as a general store. The new enterprise, however, was a failure and the man sought the Master's advice. Nityananda's advice was simple—the man should follow his true avocation and not be swayed by external considerations. In speaking to his devotee, he used the word *dandha* in referring to the duty a person must perform in this lifetime.

Lastly, there was a boy who wanted to become a pilot. When his devotee parents disapproved, he appealed to Nityananda—who took the son's side. The Master told the parents not to worry about his safety. Accidents, he said, were more likely to occur on the ground. But another crisis arose when, during the boy's eye examination, doctors detected a condition that inevitably would lead to blindness. In despair, the boy returned to Ganeshpuri where, again, Nityananda said not to worry. He then gave him a small bottle of oil to massage regularly onto his scalp. And three months later, when he retook the eye exam he was declared completely fit.

M.D. Suvarna, who took most of the later photographs of Nityananda, remembers one of the more remarkable visitors to Kailas. Swami Chinmayananda first came for darshan sometime around 1956. He returned often and frequently spoke of Nityananda to his own disciples, always calling him the living *stithaprajna* of the Bhagavad Gita—one who never wavers from consciousness. One day in 1960 he decided to take his students to Ganeshpuri. Organizing a group of musicians for the occasion, the Master received them with the honor due a visiting religious dignitary. He first invited Swami Chinmayananda to address the combined assembly from a terrace of the newly opened Bangalorewalla building and then told the swami to use the wisdom and power of Saraswati to spread the message of the Upanishads. Humbly, Swami Chinmayananda replied that he and the others present were spiritual infants compared to the great yogi. He also said that anyone attempting to describe Nityananda to the world would be trying to write "a saga of one hundred Christs living together, each exhibiting his wondrous powers to ameliorate the sufferings of the poor."

Physically, Nityananda was showing signs of age. By 1957 his teeth had deteriorated so much that two devotees threatened to fast if he did not have them removed. He finally agreed but, refusing the then typical anesthetic injection of cocaine, experienced considerable pain and bleeding. When the two devotees later offered him some food, he refused. "How can one eat when the teeth have just been removed?" he said. "You may not realize it, but yogis do experience pain. The difference is they pay it no heed."

༄

The relationship between the spiritual and physical was sublimely simple—at least for Nityananda. When some devotees complained that travel conditions and old age hindered them from more frequent visits, he countered that his physical presence was unnecessary for their spiritual growth. "Devotees will find this one wherever they meet and talk. Fish are born, live, and die in the holy Ganges without attaining liberation, but devotees have only to think of the guru." He had been saying this for years.

And when asked about the benefits of performing selfless service, the Master would reply, "Who wants it? God? Of course not—people only do it to get something in return. You should dutifully do your own work to the best of your ability without seeking a reward. That is the highest *seva* you can render. The only thing required for spiritual growth is a detachment from worldly pleasures. If you don't listen to this, you will fail in the end."

One day a devotee saw that Nityananda's feet were extremely swollen and asked about it. "People come here for some benefit," he told her, "and then leave their desires and difficulties at this one's feet. While the Ocean of Divine Mercy washes away most of these tensions, a little is absorbed by this body—a body assumed only for their sake."

༄

Whenever Nityananda intervened on a devotee's behalf, he always gave destiny the upper hand. During the monsoon of 1959, a long line of devotees and petitioners waited outside for their turn to enter the ashram. The wife of an old Gujarati devotee pleaded with Suvarna to be allowed inside.

As the doorkeeper was about to open the doors, Nityananda shouted at him to stop—and he did. But as the woman kept calling through the window and Nityananda continued shouting at him, Suvarna grew agitated. Throwing open the doors, he nervously admitted a group that included the Gujarati couple. She waited until the others had departed and then begged Nityananda to heal her husband, who was obviously gravely ill. He was silent for some time before saying, "Take him first to the hot springs and then to the dispensary for an injection." Greatly relieved, the woman thanked the Master and, half carrying her husband, left. However, en route to the kunds she spotted the dispensary and, deciding it more convenient to stop there first, took her husband inside for his injection. They then proceeded to the hot springs where, upon entering the water, the old man died.

It was in the early 1920s, following his studies in England, that Dr. M. B. Cooper received from a Himalayan saint the secret preparation for a drug with broad curative properties. The doctor spent the next decades studying the compound, which yielded astounding results. In 1959, after hearing his friend and colleague Dr. Deodhar speak of Nityananda, Dr. Cooper asked to accompany him to Ganeshpuri. He wanted to talk to the yogi about the future of the drug.

Arriving, they found Nityananda seated in his room. Dr. Cooper gazed in silence as tears streamed down his face. After a time Dr. Deodhar led him away to a restaurant where, over a cup of tea, he reminded his friend about mentioning the drug. Dr. Cooper shook his head. "You come here so often," he said, "that you only see his outer form. But I saw a dazzling crystal in his head! In a split second I was overwhemed at his purity and acutely aware of my own separation from the Divine. I could only stand before him and cry."

❧

Dr. Cooper was correct. Nityananda's unconcern with his physical body was reflected in his devotees constant awareness of it. And they were perplexed. By 1945, although he ate very little, the yogi was clearly—and mysteriously—putting on weight. In those days overnight guests cooked for themselves, always offering something to Nityananda—who declined more often than not. In fact, meals were not organized in the ashram until the early 1950s when the old west room was converted to a simple kitchen. Nonetheless, by 1960 his body had grown to huge proportions. His eating habits had not changed. If anything, now being toothless, he ate less.

Alarmed, four devotees finally voiced their concern. The first was Sandow Shetty, who as a youth had been fond of gymnastics and feats of strength. The Master told him that his heaviness was due to lack of exercise. The second inquirer was Rao, who will be recalled as suffering from chronic malaria. Nityananda told him that his swollen stomach was a result of a malaria-induced enlarged spleen. The third devotee, a practitioner of pranayama breathing exercises, was told his size was a result of breath retention. Finally Mrs. Muktabai came to him full of concern for his health and comfort. To her he said that the love of his devotees had settled around his gigantic belly. Regardless of cause, by the time Nityananda took mahasamadhi in August 1961 he was once again thin.

❧

Feeding the poor was a standard occurrence at Kailas because the food offerings brought by visitors to Ganeshpuri were distributed to local poor children. In later years, as the number of devotees grew, so did the piles of flowers and fruit baskets. Most were distributed as usual, but Nityananda allowed some to rot and then ordered them buried. One day Sandow Shetty ventured to ask about this apparent waste. He was told, "It does not go to waste. Those for whom it is meant are consuming it."

In 1958 Nityananda asked that the poor children of Ganeshpuri be fed on a permanent basis. And it was done. Within three years a hundred children a day were receiving morning meals; within twenty years the numbers surpassed 700. Today, besides the children, meals are served several times monthly to the region's *adivasi*, nearly 2,500 tribal people shunned by other communities. The ashram coffers are always full, not surprisingly, with unsolicited donations for food.

ELEVEN

Nityananda's Passing
August 8, 1961

On the afternoon of July 25, 1961, a weakened Nityananda asked Gopalmama, his attendant, to arrange for a chair to carry him to the nearby Bangalorewalla building. He said he would remain there a fortnight, and exactly two weeks later the yogi took mahasamadhi. His bed still stands in the building's main hall and is revered as a shrine.

~

Confusion was evident in the months preceding his passing. One rumor had Nityananda moving to the city of Bangalore, a plan primarily fostered by Lakshmansa Khoday, who oversaw construction of the Bangalorewalla building. He went so far as to charter an airplane. Hearing of this, devotees rushed to Ganeshpuri to argue that it would make Nityananda less accessible to them. Nityananda said he had no intention of leaving and that "an assembly of sages" had already suggested that "it be here only." But unable—or unwilling—to understand the implications of this statement, Khoday and others continued with their plans. The day before the scheduled flight, however, the Master developed diarrhea and the trip was canceled.

In hindsight, his move to the Bangalorewalla building appeared premeditated. It was the only building in Ganeshpuri large enough to encompass the multitude who would soon come to see him one last time. Remodeling the old ashram was likewise timely. In early June Nityananda learned that it was still unfinished; the voluntary backers had postponed the roof until after the monsoon season. But the yogi insisted that there was no time to lose. He ordered them to lay the slab immediately and to use ashram funds if necessary. These instructions were followed, and it was in the rebuilt section of the old Viakunt ashram that his earthly remains were later interred.

Of the many signs revealed to devotees in those last months, most were misinterpreted or ignored. For instance, Mrs. Muktabai recalled that shortly after his move to the Bangalorewalla building, Nityananda told her there would be a major pilgrimage to Ganeshpuri in two week's time. She wondered, but never thought to ask, why so many people would come during the monsoon. However, one person understood—a woman devotee from Dadar called Mataji by her followers and Mantrasiddhibai by Nityananda.

In May 1961, the day before she arrived for a visit, he experienced a discharge from his ear. He did not complain and the secretion was odorless, but devotees nonetheless called in a respected specialist. Although he had never met his patient, the doctor prostrated himself and refused to prescribe any medication until Nityananda promised to recover. The Master nodded his assurance and the doctor gave Gopalmama some capsules with instructions for administering them. He then departed. The yogi accepted a capsule, saying he did so because the good doctor had shown great sensitivity. But later he refused a second one. "One is enough," he explained. "His *bhavana* has worked." Mantrasiddhibai, learning of the discharge, began crying and begged Nityananda not to leave. She interpreted it as a sign that he was cleansing his system of toxins—and for only one purpose. The Master admonished her, "Why cry? Stop it. Greater work is possible in the subtle plane than in the gross." To the others, including Mrs. Muktabai, he said he had injured his ear long ago in a fall in the Kanheri caves.

The way Dr. Pandlaskar heard of the mahasamadhi was decidedly odd. Early that morning the doctor's nine-year-old son had confronted his parents with the words: "What are you doing here? Go to Ganeshpuri. He leaves today because the assembly of sages says that he alone can help in the forthcoming *ashtagraha* yoga. Astrological indications are for great evil to the world in general and to India in particular." The parents were so astonished at the boy's bizarre words that they reprimanded him for talking nonsense. But that evening they heard of Nityananda's passing and departed at once. The boy was so affected by his experience that he did not fully recover for years. His message was thought to refer to the conjunction of all planets in a single sign, the next occurrence being in February 1962 when all eight entered Capricorn, the sign of India.

༄

It was a hot May afternoon in 1961 when M.U. Hatengdi first heard what he called a telepathic bell announcing that Nityananda would soon take mahasamadhi. This is his story:

Fearing the yogi had already discarded his human form, I tried not to think about it. The next morning I reluctantly opened the Delhi paper even though it would hardly mention a nonpolitical event in Bombay. All the same I was relieved to find nothing in the obituaries. The prospect haunted me for the next three months. I grew insecure about my own spiritual practice even though Nityananda had told me there was nothing to read or study. But even worse was the thought of being unable to contact him in a physical form. I had not yet heard of his assurance that greater work was possible on the subtle plane, and since 1948 my visits to see him were infrequent and largely in the public eye. No longer did I quietly sit with him in private. True, he once said that when a child learns to walk the mother, still watchful, must allow it freedom to run around. Perhaps he should have added, even if the child tries to hang on to the mother! I knew his grace was with me wherever I was stationed in the Navy—but I also knew that I could contact him if necessary.

Unable to leave the naval station, I made a plan. Knowing that Mrs. Muktabai still went to Ganeshpuri every two weeks, I wrote asking her to report on Nityananda's health after each visit and enclosed some self-addressed envelopes. Her letters began arriving regularly, the first few indicating that he was well. Her third or fourth letter, however, referred to some debility as well as talk of his undertaking a trip to Kanhangad. This confused but did not worry me. He had told me in 1944 that he would remain in Ganeshpuri ashram, and even if he changed his mind, I was used to traveling great distances to see him. Besides, I was planning a visit in early August and it was then mid-July. But my anxiety continued and it was an unhappy period for me. The last letter from

Mrs. Muktabai was dated August 4 and reached me on August 7. It was a dark and rainy evening and I grew despondent reading it. She wrote me to come at once because the Master was very weak.

Back in December I had made a small altar in my home. On a corner shelf lit by the first rays of the morning sun I kept a framed photograph of Nityananda along with flowers from our garden and a silver lamp. The lamp held just enough oil to burn for an hour and it was my custom to light it every evening at sunset. The day after the distressing letter I came home for lunch to find the little lamp already burning. In turn, the picture was decorated with flower garlands and flanked by two vases, each containing eight blue water lilies. Before it was a tray of sweets traditionally prepared on the festival of Ganesh's birth. When I asked my wife why she had arranged such a display, she said she had simply felt like it. I had never shared with her my fears about Nityananda's passing and so her demonstration was all the more remarkable. She lit the oil lamp at nine that morning and it had never gone out. She collected every flower in the garden including the water lilies, something she had never done before, and then prepared the *modaks*—all this without knowing why. The mystery was solved the next morning when I learned of the mahasamadhi. While I was so absorbed in the world, the Master sent this sign of his blessing from nine hundred miles away.

⁂

Nityananda occupied a room directly above the entrance of the Bangalorewalla building. For the first three or four days, though weak, he walked a little. July 27 was his last Guru Purnima, a day on which Hindus traditionally honor the teacher, and he addressed the assembled devotees for nearly 45 minutes in a surprisingly strong voice. He said that the boxcars of a train going up a hill might slip backward without sand thrown on the tracks for traction. To maintain a lasting connection with the engine, each boxcar must forge a bond of unshakable faith and conviction. Everything else he said would happen automatically. He then mentioned plans for building a hospital in Ganeshpuri.

A day or so later, with only Madhumama present, he stood on the balcony watching the sun set in a sky that was unusually clear for July. Nityananda said, "Anyone wanting to see the sun should do it now for tomorrow he may not be seen." The following morning dawned cloudy and stayed that way as a noticeably weaker Nityananda was moved to the main hall. There he stayed until he died.

On August 7 around four in the afternoon he asked for B. H. Mehta, popularly called Babubhai Lokhandwalla. Mehta, who was in a restaurant having tea at the time, learned of the summons and hurried to the main hall. There the yogi handed him a large parcel wrapped in a piece of cloth and asked him to look after Kanhangad. The bundle contained cash, gold, and other valuables that Mehta eventually used, along with funds he collected, to build the two Kanhangad temples above the rock-cut caves and at Guruvana.

***

For months devotees had noticed in Nityananda a growing sadness that often approached tears. We can only surmise that the great yogi felt as Krishna did in the Bhagavad Gita when he said he granted supplicants what they prayed for. But more often than not, the only thing they wanted was worldly success or material gain. Too many fools, he said, passed his dwelling without asking for the liberation he offered. Likewise people brought Nityananda their earthly cares. These he relieved hoping to inspire in them a hunger for the spiritual gifts he was empowered to bestow. But in the end, like Krishna, he was disappointed. Some people actually came to Ganeshpuri for a lucky number to gamble on. They might count, for instance, how many of his fingers were visible at a given moment or the number of steps he took. Usually this was when Nityananda threw stones or shouted.

❧

On the evening of August 7 the engineer Hegde felt drawn to Ganeshpuri. Traveling alone, he gained entry to the samadhi hall with some difficulty and found Monappa at Nityananda's bedside. The doctor had just announced that there was no need to worry and was walking out with Sandow Shetty—when he dropped his medical bag with a thud. Opening his eyes, the Master asked what the noise was and then inquired who was at his feet. Hearing that it was Hegde, he told Monappa to leave. Hegde started to massage the Master's feet and was alone with him until four that morning. A little after midnight Nityananda startled him by speaking:

> People only come here for money, and the more they get the more they want. Their greed is boundless. Sometimes they arrive hungry and with only the clothes on their backs but soon they start demanding luxuries like cars and houses. One would think that with their basic human needs satisfied, they would seek something higher. Something spiritual. But they persist. There is little point in allowing this body to continue. Tomorrow I will take samadhi.

This last sentence he repeated three times. Hegde was stunned because, while Nityananda was very weak, doctors had found nothing clinically wrong with him. Most devotees fully expected him to recover. Soon he began calling for Swami Janananda, demanding to know why he had not come. When Hegde begged him to postpone his mahasamadhi, Nityananda replied that he would if asked by someone with selfless devotion and love. After all, was not Pundalika a great devotee who made the Lord of Pandharpur wait for him? And was there no such person here? One would be enough to put off the samadhi. With such a person present, he said, not even God could leave without permission. He would be unable to break that bond of pure love. And pointing his index finger at Hegde, Nityananda asked, "Can you offer this one selfless devotion?" But Hegde tearfully replied, "I don't know."

※

In the remaining hour or so, Nityananda asked for certain other devotees by name but they arrived too late. He told Hegde not to worry, and at a quarter to four again muttered something about Swami Janananda, who also came too late and only after receiving a telegram. Hegde asked if he could help but Nityananda said he needed a sanyasi. At around four o'clock he sent the engineer to bathe. Returning, Hegde offered to pour some coffee into the Master's mouth but the devotee in the next room woke up and told him to stop, saying that his plan was to bathe and then prepare Nityananda's coffee himself. And the yogi waved the engineer aside. But when the other devotee went for his bath, Hegde ran down to the hotel and asked the grateful manager to prepare some special coffee. Quickly Hegde carried it back, served it to

Nityananda, and then departed, leaving him in the care of the others wishing to attend him. Among them, sometime after seven, were several women devotees from the early days, including Mrs. Wagle, a professional nurse.

In the early days Nityananda had served sugar cane juice to visitors. When Mrs. Muktabai had once asked why, he said, "Why? Because it is this one's juice." However, that morning Nityananda requested coffee and food for those present, something he had been doing for several months. Coming from Bangalore, Lakshmansa Khoday arrived around this time.

Among those assembling since six that morning was Chandu, a longstanding devotee who had come some days before. When Nityananda suddenly asked him for some kasthuri, a type of musk oil, Chandu began to weep. Years ago in Kanhangad he had told the devotee that before leaving this world he would ask him for kasthuri. In an attempt to calm him, Nityananda asked his old companion if he knew of a train that could carry them to Kanhangad. Chandu answered, yes, there was a scheduled train. But when the yogi asked, "How can this one go without strength in these legs?," Chandu was silent.

C. C. Parekh had arranged for a lift to Bombay. He planned to leave by seven that morning, tell his staff that he would remain in Ganeshpuri a few more days, and return to the ashram that afternoon. However, as he entered the car, he suddenly stopped. Asking his friend to wait, he hurried to the hall—where he was shocked to find the Master struggling to breathe. He administered oxygen at once and Nityananda's breathing improved, but Parekh decided not to leave. Remaining at the head of the bed, he was soon joined by Dr. Nicholson, a devotee and respected eye specialist from Bombay. Dr. Nicholson's wife joined them shortly, having telephoned a doctor at the neighboring sanatorium. Soon he arrived, examined Nityananda, and prescribed some medicine. But it was too late. Nityananda had them remove the oxygen mask and, breathing normally, asked Parekh for some water. Then at a quarter of nine he asked Lakshmansa Khoday for some lemon juice. Khoday offered him fresh coconut milk instead, which he accepted. He took nothing more.

At nine-thirty Gopalmama noticed that Nityananda's body was radiating a lot of heat. Speaking for the last time, he repeated what he had said often that summer: "A sadhu became a swami. The swami became a *deva* to some, a *baba* and a *bhagawan* to others. This deva will now enter constant samadhi." Ten minutes later he took several very deep breaths, the final one expanding his chest fully. He straightened his legs, the one arthritic, as far as he could, clasped his hands above his navel, and lay perfectly still. After a time Parekh called Swami Muktananda and others from the adjoining room to take charge of Nityananda's body.

❦

Between that afternoon and the following evening, there was much discussion about where to inter the holy remains. The devotee responsible for the Kailas ashram's construction proposed building a subterranean room there. Other devotees suggested a site on the hill behind the present museum building. Another group wanted it to be where the yogi's body now rested in the Bangalorewalla building, a proposal that Khoday offered to oversee. However, the site ultimately chosen for the samadhi shrine was the recently reconstructed old ashram building. Nityananda had always said that sages gathered there, and it was remembered with what urgency he had ordered the slab roof installed during that summer's monsoon.

❧

On the morning of August 9 Captain Hatengdi arrived at his office to find a telephone message. Calling home, he learned that Mrs. Muktabai had sent a telegram saying that Nityananda had taken mahasamadhi the day before and interment would be in three days. He somehow managed to reach Bombay at eleven that night only to learn that the ceremony would occur the next morning. At that hour there were no trains or taxis and he spent a dismal night waiting for the morning train, which he caught. He pulled into Bassein, now the Vasai Road, around five-thirty to find 150 other people stranded en route to Ganeshpuri. The state transport office was still closed and the area was deserted—except for a growing crowd of anxious devotees. Captain Hatengdi joined the line, resigned to what seemed inevitable. He was 25 miles away and would never arrive in time to see Nityananda one last time.

As he stood musing, five people stepped out of line to flag down a solitary taxi. But the driver refused to make the trip and they trudged back to the throng. By now the hopelessness of the situation drove Hatengdi to pace up and down—from the station to the fork in the road. To the right lay Ganeshpuri; to the left, Bassein and the fort. Pacing this 200-yard stretch several times, he again came to the fork in the road. This time, however, he saw an old but empty seven-seat vehicle approaching from Bassein. He hailed the driver, who agreed to take Hatengdi and six other devotees who quickly piled in. The driver kept remarking on their good fortune. It seemed he rarely came this way and had been surprised to find himself at the fork in the road. At seven-fifteen he dropped them off at the Bhadrakali temple.

Captain Hatengdi, overjoyed to be there, had no idea where to find Nityananda's body. He managed to push through the crowd and five minutes later saw the body being carried from the Bangalorewalla building and placed on a jeep. At that moment the sun broke through the drizzle to light up the Master's face and Hatengdi rushed forward to catch hold of the vehicle. The hour-long procession would circle the buildings before proceeding to the old ashram's eastern entrance. As the entourage slowly began to move, the sun seemed to bow out and the drizzle resumed. The body had been arranged in the lotus position and sat in an easy chair conveyed by means of two logs tied to the chair arms. Hatengdi did not release his hold on the jeep until the chair was lowered and carried into the low building.

The old ashram was filled to capacity and there was no possibility of entering. So Hatengdi went first to bathe and then to pray. By now he knew the samadhi shrine was situated right where he used to sleep following the ashram's move to Kailas. He finally and truly understood Nityananda's earlier words to him that "this spot alone was good."

~

Nityananda's life exemplified nondualism. He made no distinction between people, never caring about their religion, their sex, or whether they were poor or wealthy, backward or educated. He was the common man's friend, the spiritual aspirant's guide, and the devotee's constant companion. He taught that devotion to God went hand in hand with the performance of one's earthly responsibilities. In fact, he demanded that people work in the world, saying that work properly done was the same as worship. He felt people should be of the world without being worldly. He particularly favored charitable works as opportunities to serve God. Always fond of feeding the poor, he built a small school in Ganeshpuri and a dispensary in Vajreshwari. Even while crediting the will of God and karmic law for the suffering of individuals and nations, he never let this justify callousness toward others.

He did not want followers. But when they came, he only asked for purity of motive and faith (*shuddha bhavana* and *shraddha*) and the freedom to do his work from within. His greatness lay in the key he held to the inner consciousness of the faithful. His power radiated without effort or notice on his part. Words were unimportant to him. Free of earthly ambition, he distributed whatever gifts people brought him. It says in the *Bhagawatam* that the divine power of such a guru remains hidden, manifesting itself for those who truly desire Truth. With Nityananda, this was so—and his manifestations were many. While emanating steadily from the spiritual plane, his divine presence reflected the viewer's inner state of consciousness. While some saw in him the terror of Kali, others found the compassion of Vajreshwari. Dualism was always unmasked as an intellectual pursuit that toyed with separate aspects of the same reality.

In his final months Nityananda complained that people only came to him for material gain. "What sort of grace is possible in such cases?" he would ask before adding, "They don't need a guru—they need a soothsayer." He called it an abuse of his physical presence, likening it to spiritual window shopping. Where was their spiritual aspiration? Why ask the ocean for a few fish when, with a little effort, one could have the priceless pearls on the ocean floor?

He spoke of the *antarjnanis*, realized beings who lived in the world and experienced pain like everyone else. The difference between them and the rest of humanity was their ability to detach their minds from their suffering. Once established in infinite consciousness, they became silent. And, while all-knowing, they lived as if knowing nothing; while manifesting simultaneously in unlikely places, they appeared idle. They viewed life as if it were a movie—from a state of detachment. For Nityananda, being detached from life's circumstances, pleasant or otherwise, was the highest state. He was an antarjnani.

Let the mind, he said, be like a lotus leaf floating on the water, unaffected by its stem below and its flower above. While engaged in worldly pursuits, keep the mind untainted by desire and distraction. Keep the mind detached and faith in God firmly established in the lotus of the heart, never letting it be swayed by happiness or dispair. Devotees will find themselves subjected to various tests, he said—tests of the mind, of the emotions, of the body. With every thought that pops into the mind, God is waiting for a person's reaction. Therefore stay alert and detached. See everything as an opportunity to gain experience, improve oneself, and rise to a higher level. Desire alone causes suffering in the world. Humankind brings nothing into this world and takes nothing away from it. This ashram, for instance, is full of things for devotees to use when visiting, but if this one [Nityananda] leaves he will take nothing with him. Whatever is needed will come. This one is not flattered when important persons come or distressed when devotees fall away. Whether visitors come or not, whether they bring offerings or not—it is the same. This one has no desire to go anywhere or see anything. Let one's thoughts and actions reflect one's words. This ashram's practice is not in doing good deeds. This ashram's practice is learning to be detached. Anything else that happens does so automatically by the will of God—although this one will speak when somebody is genuinely interested.

TWELVE

Afterword

The Shrines of Ganeshpuri

Since ancient times Ganeshpuri was considered a holy place and Nityananda often recounted episodes from the ancient Puranas attesting to this. Of the area's numerous shrines, several were built and maintained by Nityananda and his followers.

The old Bhimeshwar temple, situated near the old ashram, was one of these. Dr. Deodhar recalled that on a visit around 1950 he noticed that the silver cobra—the Naag—was missing from the temple's *linga*. But he kept forgetting to tell Nityananda. This continued for some time until one day he asked another devotee to mention it for him. Hearing the belated news, Nityananda said, "Have you come here just to tell me this? Deodhar always forgets! Tell him I said to have the Naag remade—but this time in copper." He then gave detailed instructions for its size and features, directing the devotee to use a thread to show the dimensions. Finally, he said he wanted it installed on the following Monday—four short days away. Receiving these instructions, the doctor hurried at once to the marketplace where he was directed to a certain artisan. This man, the district's only coppersmith, announced the project would take him ten days to complete. Anxiously, Dr. Deodhar explained the urgency and the coppersmith agreed to finish it by Sunday.

When he arrived to pick up the Naag, the doctor saw that the cobra's eyes did not glisten as instructed. The coppersmith explained he had left off the shiny beads, fearing they would fall out and leave empty sockets. At that moment a statue of Shiva was carried in from the workshop, its eyes brightly painted and shiny. The men looked at it and decided to do the same for the snake. Nityananda was satisfied with the results and kept it in his room until the installation, which occurred the next morning.

An unusual feature of the Bhimeshwar temple was the continuous trickle of water from the ceiling at the rear of the dome. It had begun seeping from a number of places behind the main linga sometime in the early 1940s after Nityananda moved to Ganeshpuri. As time passed the amount of water increased, even during the hot summers. Captain Hatengdi heard this from his uncle who added that Nityananda had cautioned him not to step on the small lingas that sprang up wherever the water fell. And indeed, two discernible lingas were forming in two water-filled holes directly behind the main linga. Projections of various shapes also appeared in a rough semicircle around them. Whenever Nityananda mentioned the water, he would laugh heartily at the thought of scientists coming to investigate the phenomenon. It is said that once the yogi left the old ashram for Kailas in 1956, the water slowed to a trickle and stopped completely the day Nityananda's statue was installed in the Samadhi Mandir temple.

On one of his monthly weekend visits in 1945, Captain Hatengdi noticed a small shrine 200 yards from the road to the ashram. Nityananda said he built it for the village deity, or *gramadevata*, because the spot had the power of samadhi. And it was here that Swami Muktananda later made his ashram.

The current Krishna temple stands where once there was an old stone relic of Nandi, the bull of Shiva. Its presence had always been a mystery. Captain Hatengdi recalls watching Nityananda sit on it occasionally, both feet dangling down its left side. When they began building the temple, workers tried to move the stone—but it would not budge. Hearing of this, Nityananda ordered them to break a coconut near the bull. Once they did, two of them easily lifted the great stone. At the Master's instructions, they then removed the bull's head, placing it on the cow statue that stands behind Krishna.

With the Krishna temple finished, Nityananda immediately turned his attention to the Bhadrakali temple. Whenever he decided to build a shrine, no time was wasted. He would set a specific day for its inauguration and the work had to be completed. In this instance, Mistry had a single day to make the goddess's statue and, per Nityananda's instructions, he used the same cement mixture employed earlier for Krishna. But when it was finished, the priest anxiously said her face was not attractive enough. This, Nityananda reassured him, would be taken care of—and ordered the statue covered with a white cloth. At the following morning's consecration ceremony the cloth was removed to reveal a changed face that satisfied even the priest's aesthetic expectations. Later, when asked why the hurry to build this particular temple, Nityananda replied that Bhadrakali had followed him from Gokarn, desiring a place in Ganeshpuri. And she was not prepared to wait!

Besides those actually built by him, numerous shrines were dedicated to Nityananda after his mahasamadhi. The first temple built on Kanhangad rock opened in April 1963, the one in Guruvana in May 1966. The rock temple was commissioned by B.H. Mehta from funds he collected.

Known as Samadhi Mandir, the samadhi shrine was the creation of Prabhashankar Sompura, who designed the renowned Somnath Temple as well as the two Kanhangad temples. The samadhi shrine with Nityananda's earthly remains is located on the site of the original Ganeshpuri ashram. Rising a hundred feet into the sky, the shrine and hall capped by a 24-foot high dome have an imposing beauty. The Tansa River flowing a short distance away adds to the tranquility of this holy site.

Additional temples dedicated to Nityananda range from simple altars adorned with his photograph to more elaborate temples such as the one built by M.L. Gupta in Koilandi near Calicut. With its large hall, this shrine sits where the young Ram once roamed with his adopted father Ishwar Iyer.

Nityananda's Photographer

Nityananda hated being photographed and only a handful of images from the early days exist. Most of the photographs we have of him were taken decades later by M.D. Suvarna.

Devotees often wanted a picture of Nityananda with their families. Typically the young Nityananda discouraged people from revering his photographs and actually admonished them for doing so. Mrs. Krishnabai felt that since he had obliged the photographer in her own compound she might be permitted to keep his picture in her house. Accordingly, she asked the photographer to send one to her mother's house. When she arrived to pick up the framed photograph, it was nighttime. Mangalore still lacked electricity in those days and with only kerosene lamps burning Mrs. Muktabai did not notice Nityananda sitting in a dark corner. As she was asking her mother about the picture, the yogi exclaimed, "So you want a photograph, do you? You will find it in the dung heap!" Running outside, she looked to no avail. It was then that her mother said Nityananda had smashed the framed picture with a rock. The shards, of course, now lay buried in the dung heap.

Photographs of Nityananda only became readily available when M.D. Suvarna, originally a press photographer, came to Ganeshpuri in the early 1950s. He and a colleague, learning of Nityananda's growing popularity, knew people would soon be demanding photographs. But when they arrived at the ashram, Nityananda thundered at them and they retreated in haste. Suvarna, however, decided to try again. This time his persistence was rewarded. Permission was granted, after considerable pleading, under the following conditions: there should be no disturbance, no fuss, no posing.

Suvarna first traveled to Ganeshpuri as a photographer but he soon became a devotee. Whenever work brought him to Bombay, he made a point of visiting Ganeshpuri on Thursdays and shooting a roll of film. The resulting images consistently portray Nityananda's mystical power, compassion, and inner bliss. Some are so good that they may be mistaken for posed portraits. Others show considerable variance

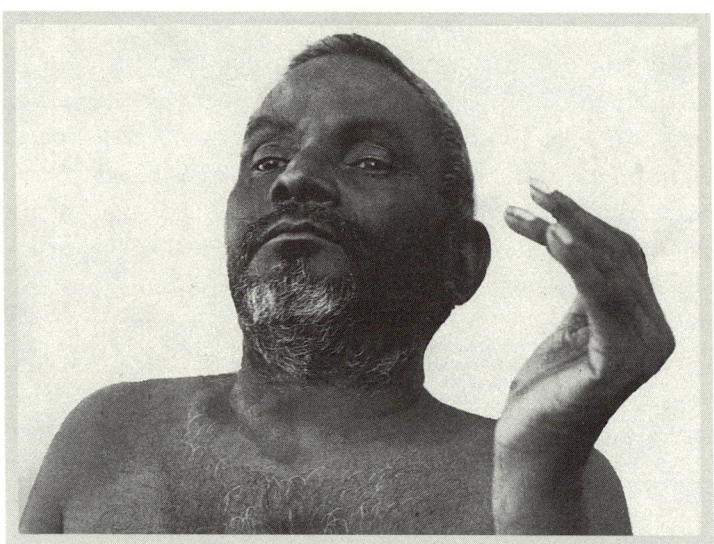

in Nityananda's physical appearance from picture to picture, a fact pointed out by the sculptor, Mr. Wagh, who utilized them for the altar statue in the samadhi shrine.

As an experiment, in the late 1950s, Mr. Suvarna exposed several hundred feet of motion picture film, taking snippets at odd moments and later splicing them together. It was the first time he had handled such a camera and his results were remarkably good. Oddly, however, on occasion the developed film was completely blank. For instance, once he wanted to photograph Nityananda returning from his morning walk. After having a hole bored in the wall of a nearby hotel, Suvarna waited with his pre-adjusted camera and took several shots of the Master passing. But the developed film was blank. He repeated the experiment—with the same result. Suvarna recalls Nityananda sometimes asking him, "What is the value of so many pictures? Are you still not satisfied?" And then he would smile.

One last time, on a particularly important occasion, Suvarna's cameras unaccountably malfunctioned. It was August 10, 1961, two days after the mahasamadhi. The body had been placed in an easy chair, mounted on a jeep, and driven slowly around the Ganeshpuri compound, a procession that, despite a steady drizzle, Suvarna managed to capture on film. Then the body was taken inside the old ashram for burial. From different vantage points in the room, Suvarna and his cousin each took a roll of film during the ceremony. But later they discovered that not one exposure came out.

Sri Nityananda Arogyashram Hospital at Ganeshpuri

The beginning of Sri Nityananda Arogyashram is in a way connected with the late Dr. M.B. Cooper and the herbal wonder drug revealed to him by a Himalayan saint long ago. Through vibrational guidance and his own genius he successfully prepared an injectable solution from the original formula, which he initially prescribed for tuberculosis. However, Dr. Cooper knew the Himalayans took it both to combat disease and to maintain health, and further research proved the compound's broader curative properties. As a result, over the years he helped patients suffering from asthma and other lung ailments, skin diseases, arthritis, cysts, as well as tuberculosis—even advanced cases. He named the remedy *mahawaz*—"the great sound"—because of the cosmic sound that seemed to direct his research.

Dr. Deodhar had been Dr. Cooper's assistant since the late 1930s. A decade later he became a devotee of Nityananda and, after seeking the Master's advice, left general practice to concentrate on mahawaz. He was told the remedy would be successful if administered through an ashram hospital but that such a project would require great patience and perseverence on his part.

Eventually, Dr. Deodhar and B.C.S. Swamy, a fellow devotee, brought Dr. Cooper to Ganeshpuri. Upon first seeing Nityananda, the doctor was overwhelmed and had to leave. But he returned later with an ampule of mahawaz to show the yogi. Again, Nityananda said it would succeed. A few months before the mahasamadhi Dr. Deodhar and Mr. Swamy presented a proposal for a hospital to be built at Ganeshpuri. Nityananda immediately approved the idea and asked for a map of the ashram's property. He indicated where he wanted the future hospital built, giving them the piece of land along with a cash donation. He said to proceed in three stages, indicating with his hands and saying, "First small, then big, and then very big!"

In 1963 the Nityananda Arogyashram Trust was formed, and in December 1966 the hospital's foundation stone was laid by Swami Chinmayananda in the presence of a distinguished audience. Today one of the district's finest hospital buildings, its spacious and airy rooms are within walking distance of the samadhi shrine.

Dr. Cooper donated the mahawaz formula to the Trust. Although he and Dr. Deodhar received fabulous offers for this formula, they were determined to maintain its availability to common people. Similarly, his daughter, Dr. M.H. Pavri, and his son, Mr. Cooper, gave up their rights to any entitled royalties. Upon the death of her father in August 1980, Dr. Pavri assumed responsibility for the hospital as well as for the manufacture and development of the herbal extract.

So Say the Stars

There is considerable interest today in Vedic astrology, an ancient science predating its Western counterpart by millenia. To this end readers may be interested in a horoscope prepared for Captain Hatengdi in March 1970. (Incidentally, the Western word "horoscope" is of ancient Greek derivation and refers to "looking at time.") In such instances, sages with intuitive wisdom chart all possible permutations and combinations to develop the pattern of a subject's life.

In India these are called Nadigrantha readings. Full of great detail, they include the names and charts of individuals influencing the subject in good or bad ways, often referring to previous incarnations. However, such readings are primarily useful in understanding a subject's past and inherent tendencies. Present and future predictions often prove unreliable because of the ongoing play of human will and divine intervention. In Captain Hatengdi's case, at the age of 28 he was shown to meet a great being who would affect his life quite favorably. There was a lengthy description of this being, which we include here in an edited form.

> He came to the world for the sake of his devotees, a great yogi. Nothing is known of his birth or his age. He has fed thousands of sanyasis and sadhus. While ever in samadhi, he talks. While ever with the Atman, he is never in the body. He talks directly to God. Long-limbed with a vibrant personality, he sometimes goes naked and sometimes wears a loincloth. Although few recognize him, he is God in human form.
>
> He is called by a name beginning with the letter N. He sits near hot springs and a Shiva temple and does not engage in outward activities, giving the impression of

doing nothing. Money he takes from his loincloth as needed. He removes difficulties and occasionally prescribes medicines. Ignorant people never see his true nature.

While these words cannot possibly relate his greatness, a devotee will come in due course and describe him properly. Others who write about him will succeed only if they are inspired by him—and then only if he wishes it. Eventually books will be written about him and many will make money in his name.

At the time of this reading, he is no longer in human form. His many devotees include highly evolved sanyasis and members of royalty. Numerous ashrams and shrines are built in his honor—but he never recognized or initiated disciples. No one was fit to receive the knowledge of God from him. Although he has taken mahasamadhi, his blessings remain with his devotees. When you think of him, he is with you. Anyone who approaches him with purity of motive is granted their wish.

How can we describe such a being? He might deliver harsh words or actions, saying "Matti, matti—it is of no consequence," but blessings always fall on the recipient. He sees with equal-sightedness, treating everyone the same regardless of social position. But people pursue him with material desires—not with spiritual aspirations. Still, his guiding light is always available to both the devout and the spiritual seeker. Sadly, most devotees never really knew him. No one was powerful enough to succeed him or receive what he could grant. But he still blesses the devotees—and he remains without disciples.

Glossary

The definitions in this glossary are limited to the specific context of this book and do not claim to be authoritative. In the case of transliteration inconsistencies between the South Indian usage followed in this text and classic Sanskrit, the Sanskrit spelling is given in italics.

acharya teacher

adivasi tribal people

ajnani one without wisdom: ignorant one

ananda literally, bliss; this is the traditional ending for names of initiates of certain orders of monks

anna daan anna: food; daan: charity or distribution

Annapoorna aspect of Mother Parvati as the Complete Feeder

antarjnani antar: inner; jnani: one who knows; one who has attained divine wisdom

arathi (sanskrit *arati*) light; the ritual of waving a light and incense before a holy picture, statue, or place

Arjuna hero of the *Mahabharata*; the teaching of the Bhagavad Gita was given to him by Krishna

arrack fermented beverage from the sap of the toddy palm; a country drink

ashirvad blessing

ashram a stage of life; retreat; a place for spiritual exercise, instruction, and practice

ashtagraha yoga astha: eight; graha: grasping, holding; as an astrological term, refers to time when all planets are aligned in one sign

ashtasiddhi ashta: eight; siddhi: literally, accomplishment; here, occult power acquired through discipline

atman Self, Absolute; also the individual self; essence

avadhuta one who is God-mad; does not keep a fixed residence, may appear eccentric, is not aware of dirt or cleanliness, of hunger or sleep; and is neither attracted nor repelled by the dualities of the phenomenal world

avatar consciously willed descent of spirit into matter; the Supreme Spirit assuming human form

Ayurveda ancient Hindu art of medicine and prolonged life; ayu: life; veda: knowledge

—bai suffix rendering a name into the feminine gender; same as —amma and —deva

Bal Bhojan literally, feeding of young boys; here refers to providing meals to poor children

Benares also *Banares* and *Banaras*; now officially called *Varanasi*; also called *Kashi*, meaning City of Light; it is a very holy place for Hindus; to die in Benares, to be burned on its sacred ghats and to have one's ashes scattered into the holy river is thought to put an immediate end to the cycles of death and rebirth, thus, liberation.

Bhadrakali a goddess

Bhagavad Gita *Divine Song;* part of the *Mahabharata*, written between 200 BC and AD 200 (dates disputed)

Bhagawan godhead; one who possesses the six treasures; one who is full of light

Bhagawatam life of Krishna written by Vyasa

bhajans devotional songs

bhakti devotion; selfless devotion to god as a means of attaining liberation

bhavana feeling; emotion, sensitivity; creative contemplation

Bhimeshwar a god; Bhima, "the mighty one," was a brother of Arjuna

Brahma vidya knowledge of God Brahman—one of the many Indian terms used to describe pure undifferentiated consciousness; the Ultimate

brahman the first and highest of the four orders of traditional Indian society; priests belong to this order

Brahmarandra literally, the opening to God in the head; the place where the spinal column meets the brain

chaddar versatile strip or square of cloth used as a shawl or blanket

chaturmas chatur: four; literally, four months; the four months of monsoon during which, traditionally, wandering sadhus would stay in one place; now a period spent in special study

Chidakash Gita title of a collection of the sayings of Nityananda; chid: consciousness compared to the sky; akash: space; Gita: song; implies a space or state in which perception is objectless

dandha literally, stick, as in "stick of justice"; in this usage refers to duty or experiences that must be lived out

darshan literally, seeing; in particular the act of seeing the divinity within the guru or within the representation of the divine as in a sculpture or painting; a system of philosophy

datta devata siddhi datta: great sage who embodies the trinity of Brahma, Vishnu, and Shiva; deva: god/goddess; siddhi: power acquired through spiritual practice

Devi literally, a shining one; goddess (deva: god)

digamber nude

drishti sight

durlabh very rare, almost impossible

Ganesha elephant-headed son of Shiva and Parvati

ghee a form of clarified butter used in Hindu rituals; also widely used in Indian cooking

Gopala form of Krishna as the cow-tender

gopi a milkmaid; Krishna danced and played with Gopis

Govinda literally, giver of enlightenment; name of Krishna

gramadevata village deity (grama: village)

Gujarat province on NW coast of India, north of Bombay

guru the teacher, especially a spiritual teacher preceptor giving personal religious instructions

Guru Purnima festival of the guru; held in July on the night of the full moon

Guruvana jungle area near Kanhangad; legend has it that the infant Nityananda was found abandoned here; today it is the site of a temple dedicated to Nityananda

Haj pilgrimage to Mecca; a Moslem holy event

halwa sweet confection common in the middle and far east

harijan untouchable

harikatha sacred story told in song and narrative; hari: god; katha: story

Indra chief god in the Vedic pantheon

Ishwara simply, Lord or deity

japa mantra repetition

jnani one who knows; wise one; one who has attained divine wisdom (*jnana*); wisdom acquired through meditation

Kailas mountain in the Himalayas called the home of Shiva; the name of Nityananda's second ashram in Ganeshpuri which he occupied from 1956 to 1961

Kali Yuga the present age; fourth in a series as given in ancient Hindu texts

kamandalu water container traditionally carried by wandering sadhus

karma action itself; action done with desire for results, the fruits of which are either being manifested or accumulated

kasthuri (Sanskrit *kasturi*) musk

koti-teertha teertha: holy place; koti: 10 million; thus, very holy places

kumkum vermilion powder used in rituals

kundalini the creative power of Shiva as it is manifested in the individual; literally, coiled up

kunds (*kunda*) hot springs; baths

langoti loincloth

linga literally, sign; short column, resembling a phallus, often with a cobra head behind it; in Hindu worship, it is a symbol of Shiva and the masculine principle

maha great

Mahabharata ancient Hindu epic collection; contains 18 books, including the Bhagavad Gita

mahapurusha purusha: person, male, one's true self; regarded as eternal and unaffected by external happenings; maha: great; indicates one who resides always in this true and unchanging self

mahasamadhi literally, great resolution, resolving; when speaking of a saint, it is the conscious shedding of the physical body

mahawaz name given by Dr. Cooper to the medicine used at the Nityananda Arogyashram hospital

mandir temple

mantra sacred word or formula to be chanted; that sacred word or formula by which the nature of the Supreme is reflected on as identical with the self

mantrasiddhi powers that arise from mantra repetition

mantravadi one who repeats mantra; one who believes in doctrine of mantra; derivatively, one who has attained extraordinary power through use of mantra repetition

math monastery

mathadipathi leader of a math; abbot

Matsyendranath great sage of the Nath order

matti literally, dust; of no consequence, useless

maya literally, that which measures; power which produces sense of difference and diverse objects; the appearance and experience of duality

modaks traditional food prepared at the feast for the birth of Ganesh

moksha absolute freedom from bondage

mukti liberation from bondage

Naag snake, particularly a cobra; seen in Shiva shrines

Nandi a bull; Shiva's vehicle

nityananda eternal bliss; nitya: constant, continuous

padmasana the lotus posture of hatha yoga; often described as an ideal seated position of meditation

para supreme (usually seen as a prefix)

parabrahma supreme deity; God

paramatma supreme soul; God

Parvati goddess; consort of Shiva

pipal a fig tree native to India; with its multiple descending roots it resembles the banyan tree of the west

pooja worship or ritual; a more modern spelling is *puja*

poorna full

prasad consecrated food given by a deity or guru to disciple; in many rituals, it is customary for devotees to bring an offering and to receive prasad in return

Puranas literally, ancient; a collection of symbolic and allegorical writings, mythological in character; there are 18 such scriptures

raddi waste material

Ramayana great epic of Hindu literature; foundation of Indian historical writing, along with the *Puranas* and *Mahabharata*

rishimandal rishi: sage; mandal: circle; assembly of sages

sadhana literally, accomplishment; pursuit of an ideal; spiritual practice or discipline

sadhu literally, good; holy man

sahitya literally, epic

samadhi literally, resolution, resolving; "drawing together of the mind" through contemplation, meditation; state of higher consciousness in which the fluctuation of the mind ceases

samartha very capable; capable in all respects

sanatkumar(s) one of the four sons of Brahma, "the Holy Youths," born of his mind alone

sankalpa literally, decide to do; a vow or resolution

sanyasi (*sannyasi*) literally, one who has cast away; a renunciate

Saraswati (a) goddess of learning and the arts; (b) river; one of three rivers that converge at Allahabad (Saraswati, Jumna, Ganga)

satpurushas sat: existence, being; purusha: one's true self

satyanarayana satya: truth; narayana: name of Vishnu; *satyanarayana pooja* is a popular ritual performed to attain certain desired results

seva selfless service

shakti the power of the absolute

Shankara great Vedantist teacher and author (9th century AD); organized 10 orders of monks and four major monasteries; the chief teacher of each monastery is known as the Shankar/acharya of (city)

shastri one who is learned in the holy books (shastras)

shishya disciple

shradda (*shraddha*) intense faith, deeper than the mind; involves both knowledge and will or dynamism

shuddha bhavana sincere feeling; purity of feeling and motive

siddhi literally, accomplishment; any occult power acquired through discipline

stithaprajna one whose knowledge is firmly established, who is always the witness; who never wavers from consciousness

swami literally, master of one's Self; title given to monks of the orders organized by Shankara

swaraj swa: self; raj: kingdom; self-rule, self-government

swayam praapti self-attained

teerthayatra pilgrimage

toddy tapper the sap of the toddy palm is collected and distilled to yield an intoxicating beverage; the person who taps the trees and collects the sap is called a toddy tapper.

tonga horse drawn carriage; still a common mode of travel in rural areas

trishula trident; symbol of the three powers of the Absolute: will, knowledge, action; often associated with Shiva

tulsi basil

Upanishads the most recent of the *Vedas*, written about 900 BC (dates disputed); the philosophical portions of the *Vedas*

vairagya distaste for and detachment from worldly values

Valmiki author of the *Ramayana*

vasana literally, smell; predilection, residual traces of action and impressions retained in the mind; habit energy

Vedas oldest scripture of Hinduism and the most ancient religious text in an Indo-European language, probably compiled between 1000 - 500 BC (dates disputed)

veera padmasana the veera pose is the hero pose; padmasana is the lotus posture

vishwaroopa form of the Absolute; universal form of god

walla suffix meaning "person in charge of, who trades in, who owns"; e.g., the ticketwalla is the person in charge of tickets

yajna Vedic sacrifice ritual or ceremony

yoga union of individual self with the Supreme Being or Ultimate Principle; also samadhi or trance

yogi one who studies and practices yoga

About the Authors

Swami Chetanananda, an American meditation master in the lineage of Nityananda, is Abbot of the Rudrananda Ashram and Director of the Nityananda Institute in Portland, Oregon. The Rudrananda Ashram is a community of people living a practical and contemporary spiritual life based on teachings and a meditation practice with roots in the ancient Kashmir Shaivite traditions of India. It is named for Swami Rudrananda (Rudi), an American spiritual teacher who was deeply influenced by his contacts with Nityananda and who was initiated into the Saraswati order of monks by Swami Muktananda. Swami Chetanananda assumed leadership of the Ashram on Rudrananda's passing in 1973. The Nityananda Institute is a not-for-profit center for meditation and quality living committed to making a spiritual life both understandable and accessible to Americans. It is named for Nityananda of Ganeshpuri.

M.U. Hatengdi was born at Mangalore in December 1914, had his early education in the local G.H. School and Government College, and obtained his Honors/Masters degree in Economics from the Presidency College, Madras in 1936.

Joining the Indian Navy in 1941, he retired in 1964. At the time of retirement, Capt. Hatengdi was the Naval Secretary at Naval Headquarters, New Delhi. He was immediately appointed as the Commercial Manager in the government-owned Mazagaon Dock and soon after was selected as the General Manager and Chairman of the Board of Administration of one of the largest buying and selling agencies of the government, known as the Canteen Stores Department, from which he retired in July 1970.

He has since been interesting himself in activities connected with social organizations and religious trust.